Will farts DESTROY the planet?

Glenn Murphy received his master's degree in science communication from London's Imperial College of Science, Technology and Medicine. He wrote his first popular science book, *Why Is Snot Green?*, while managing the Explainer team at the Science Museum in London. In 2007 he moved to the United States. He now lives and works in Raleigh, North Carolina, with his wife, Heather, and two unusually large and ill-tempered cats.

Favourite science fact: the eye of a colossal squid measures 27 cm (almost a foot) across. It has the largest eyes of any animal in the world.

Will farts DESTROY the planet?

and other extremely important questions
(and answers) about climate change
from the Science Museum

Glenn Murphy

Illustrated by Mike Phillips

MACMILLAN CHILDREN'S BOOKS

First published 2011 by Macmillan Children's Books

This edition published 2013 by Macmillan Children's Books
an imprint of Pan Macmillan
20 New Wharf Road, London N1 9RR
Associated companies throughout the world
www.panmacmillan.com

ISBN 978-1-4472-5135-4

Text copyright © Glenn Murphy 2011
Illustrations copyright © Mike Phillips 2011

The right of Glenn Murphy and Mike Phillips to be identified as
the author and illustrator of this work has been asserted by them
in accordance with the Copyright, Designs and Patents Act 1988.

3 5 7 9 8 6 4

A CIP catalogue record for this book is available from
the British Library.

Typeset by Perfect Bound Limited
Printed and bound by CPI Group (UK) Ltd, Croydon, CR0 4YY

Contents

Thanks to . . .

Gaby Morgan and all at Macmillan Children's Books for their continued support.

Deborah Bloxam (sorry, Patterson – congrats!), Stuart Umbo, and everyone on the Science Museum Climate Change gallery team who offered their help, support and comments.

Dr Roger Blackmore of the Open University for keeping me in line, and for his many great comments and suggestions. Any mistakes that remain are mine, but in any case, this book is all the better for your efforts!

Patric Lane, Professor John Bruno, Dr Lauren Buckley and Dr Tamlin Pavelsky at the University of North Carolina, for invaluable help, advice and steerage.

Jake, Larry and Beth Sherrill – the inspiration for Jake and his folks in the story.

Sarah Burthe – still on the grubby, freezing front lines of science.

Heath Murphy – the inimitable Bruv'nor, and all-round top bloke.

Alyse Campbell – cutest baby in the western hemisphere. And quite possibly the other one too.

As always, the Murphs, the Witts, Heather and the fuzzies. Bug luv to you all.

Foreword: how this book works

This is not a textbook. You don't need to study it, memorize it, or answer its questions for homework. Unless, of course, you really *want* to . . .

This is a book that tells two stories.

The first is an imaginary tale about a boy named Jake, set around the year 2050. The story follows Jake as he explores the history of climate change for a school project.

Sound like fun to you?

No?

But remember this – Jake's history is our future. So along the way he'll be whizzing through our future traffic, exploring our future cities, talking to our future computers and eating our future foods. And while the story is fictional, everything in it is based on what scientists and engineers say *could* happen in the not-so-distant future.

The second tale is not imaginary.

It's the real story of climate change on planet Earth. It explains what's happening to the planet *right now*. It tells us all about climate science, and what we do and don't know about our environment, and why it's changing. And it looks at how we might adapt our lives and technologies to survive in a changing world.

We'll meet robot cars and high-speed supertrains, solar houses and drinkable toilets, future farms and farting cows, and, by the end of it, you'll know so much about climate change and future technology, you'll be able to do

Jake's homework for him! But happily, you won't have to. No tests, no essays – just read, enjoy and learn.

Also, you can read this book however you like.

Each section begins with part of Jake's fictional future story and then goes on to explore the real ideas and technologies Jake discovers along the way. But you don't have to read it all start-to-finish. You might prefer to skip between the chapters and read all the story bits first, then go back and read the 'real' stuff later. Or you might want to browse the chapters like web pages, dipping in and out wherever you feel like it. It's up to you.

But before you get stuck in, here's a quick introduction to climate science – just so you know where to start . . .

Introduction to Climate Science

Climate change isn't easy to get your head around. While the basic idea is pretty simple, the science can be complicated and confusing. What's more, people always seem to be arguing about how it works, how to tackle it, and whether it needs worrying about at all.

In the scientific world, pretty much everyone agrees that climate change is real, that it's happening right now and that it's definitely worth worrying about. But there are still questions about how quickly it's happening, how to stop it or slow it down, what problems it will lead to, how it will affect our future world and who will be affected.

The truth is, there is still a great deal we don't know about climate change. Predicting how it will affect the planet is a bit like predicting the weather – the further ahead you try to look, the harder it gets.

You might have noticed that weather forecasters on different channels on TV sometimes come up with different forecasts for the weather a week from now. But they almost always agree on what will happen tomorrow. Climate scientists are a bit like that, only they work on much longer timescales.

Just like weather forecasters, they measure temperatures, gas pressures and other features of the atmosphere and oceans, and use them to build computer models of how the climate is likely to change in the future. And while two different scientists might come up with different ideas of what will happen 500 years from now, they almost always agree on what will happen in fifty.

This book, then, is based on what the majority of climate scientists say is likely to happen to the world within the next few decades.

The good news is that we're not talking about global disasters just yet. The oceans are not going to flood the entire planet. Ice caps and glaciers will (mostly) still be around, and most of the world's plants and animals – including us – will happily survive to see the next century.

The bad news is, there will be changes. Ice will melt, waters will rise, temperatures will rise, and people, plants and animals worldwide will be affected in a whole host of different ways.

So what do scientists think is happening? Well, here's the short version:

1) The atmosphere on our planet is already warmer than it should be, thanks to the greenhouse effect.
As you might already know, water vapour, carbon dioxide, methane and other gases in the Earth's atmosphere trap heat and keep the planet warmer than they should be, given that it's quite a long way from the Sun. Without the greenhouse effect, the Earth would be a much, much colder place, and most living things (including us) simply could not survive on it.

2) Our climate can change naturally over very long periods of time.
Global temperatures go up and down naturally over periods ranging from centuries to millions of years. This can happen after large asteroid impacts and volcanic

eruptions, or as the Earth's orbit of the Sun shifts or due to changes in the Sun's brightness or interactions between oceans, atmosphere and ice.

3) But the world now seems to be warming much faster than it should.
During the last fifty years especially, the warming of the atmosphere and oceans has sped up. A lot. And neither volcanoes nor asteroids, changes in the Sun or changes in our orbit around it can explain how quickly and by how much these temperatures are rising.

4) This recent warming seems to be man-made – caused by our burning massive amounts of fossil fuels for power and energy.
We've been burning coal, oil and gas for heat, light and energy to power machines for centuries. But it's only in the last hundred years or so that we've started burning HUGE amounts of them. Since 1900 the world's population has exploded, and with it the number of farms, factories and vehicles needed to support all those billions of people. Every new machine burns more fossil fuels and adds more greenhouse gases (like methane and carbon dioxide) to the atmosphere. Over time this has built up, changing our atmosphere and warming our planet in new and unusual ways.

So now we know all this, what are we going to do about it?
Well, that's what the rest of this book is all about. How *much* the world will change – and how much we'll be affected – will partly depend on what we do *now*.
Right now the warming of the atmosphere and oceans

shows no signs of slowing down. And while we have noticed it, and taken some steps to tackle it, we're still burning thousands of tonnes of fossil fuels and releasing thousands of tonnes of methane and carbon dioxide into the atmosphere every year. Even if we stopped burning fossil fuels *right now*, the warming would still continue fifty or one hundred years from now because there's already so much heat-trapping carbon dioxide in the atmosphere from the past 150 years of fossil-fuel use. And it doesn't seem likely that the world is going to stop burning fossil fuels any time soon.

Happily, though, we *are* doing things to try to tackle the problem. We're inventing new energy-saving technologies. We're developing new cleaner fuels and energy sources that might one day help get the atmosphere back to where it was. Now it's just a question of how quickly we can make it all come about.

We can't know for sure what will happen in our world by the year 2050, or what the kids and adults of the future will think about our efforts to deal with climate change today. This book represents one possible vision of how it might turn out.

The best thing you can do for our future world is to be like Jake, the hero of our story. Like Jake, you should ask questions, get answers and find out all you can about climate change and what can be done about it. That way, you'll be ready for the future, no matter what it brings.

OK – are you ready?

Then it's time to go. Off to the year 2050, where the school day is just ending . . .

1. Transport and Travel

Jake left school in a huff. As the bright, cheery digital chimes signalled the end of the school day, he hefted his laptop-backpack and stomped towards the huge solar-glass walls of the entrance lobby.

Frowning hard, he swung an angry foot at the clear exit doors. But of course they slid harmlessly aside with a quiet hiss, well before his foot could make contact. This just made him angrier. It was as if the school itself was mocking him, wasting his time, laughing at him.

This, for Jake, was not an unusual feeling. He had never really liked school and didn't see why he had to go. After all, some kids didn't. More and more kids these days were at Virtual Schools – joining classes via webcam and doing all their work from home. *Those* kids didn't have to deal with beefy meatheads beating them up in PE classes. *Those* kids didn't have to worry about the 'cool gangs' giggling at them because their clothes and hair weren't trendy enough.

Jake was more short, dark and thoughtful than tall, tough and trendy. He found his daily school-work easy, if hardly exciting. He could happily do it all at home, on the screen of his touchscreen computer – one window open for his geography test, and three more for chatting and gaming with his friends.

Besides, going to school was just a waste of time. Jake wanted to be a games designer. What could easy, boring maths and geography classes teach him about that? He was just biding his time until he could leave school for DigiTech College. Then he'd be happy and free – like his big brother. Heath was at university already. No one bothered *him* about getting *his* homework done.

Jake was still frowning and grumbling as he stomped across the wide, flat square in front of the school and into the leafy park that lay beyond. Bike-riders and other walkers wove around him as he strode onward to the meeting place by the fountain.

Jake's dad worked in a small office less than a

mile from the school. So he and Jake would drive into town together each day, park the car, walk together for ten minutes or so until they reached the park, then split up at the fountain to walk the last part of their journeys. At the end of each day they'd meet back at the fountain to make the reverse trip home. Dad said it saved energy, and that the walking did them good. Dad was like that. Always going on about saving water and energy and stuff.

So today – like every day – Jake arrived at the fountain to find his dad there waiting for him.

'Hey, son,' said Dad, 'why the long face?'

'Hrrmph,' offered Jake by way of an answer, not stopping to wait as he strode past the fountain.

'I see,' said Dad, falling into step beside him. For a minute they walked in silence down the long, tree-lined path leading back to the parking centre. But Jake couldn't stand this for long.

'It's this *stupid* homework project,' he blurted. 'I have to do it this week, and email it to Mr Sharp by Friday morning. It'll take *ages* to do. And Dave and I just got to level twelve on *World of Ninja Dragoncraft*! It's such a pain. My whole week is ruined.'

'OK . . . ' said Dad warily. 'So what's the project about?'

They were walking on over the wide footbridge connecting the park to the parking centre, passing over the buzzing lanes of cars, buses and bikes below.

'It's about how the world dealt with climate change, from 2000 to 2050. Like, *ancient* history-of-science stuff. We have to find out all the big changes that happened in those fifty years. Like how they cleaned up transport, how they changed the way they make and use energy, how they dealt with the water crisis back in the twenties, and how plant and animal life has adapted to a warmer planet.'

'Wow. That's quite a list.'

'Exactly! It's just not fair.'

'Anything else?'

'Yeah. We also have to draw up this timeline of big 'turning points' in history. Like when the USA, UNASUR*, Russia, China and India signed some big Carbon Treaty or something. Bo-o-o-o-ring.'

They arrived at the bottom deck of the parking centre and hopped into the cylindrical glass-walled

---

* The Union of South American Nations (Union de NAciones SURamericanas). This is an organization of South and Central American nation-states – including Brazil, Argentina, Columbia, Peru and others. It was founded in 2008, and by 2025 it had become larger and more powerful than the USA

Up-Shuttle that would take them to level five. The doors slid shut, and the shuttle sped smoothly upwards.

'Well, you know,' said Dad a little testily, 'to *some* people that's not such ancient history. And to *some* people those turning points were very important and exciting.' The doors slid open and they emerged right in front of Dad's shiny silver Nissan ElectroRailer.

'Whatever,' said Jake, shrugging off his backpack and slumping into the passenger seat. As the electric motor silently started, and the car began its smooth glide around the spiralling ramp down to ground level, Jake stared huffily out of the window, his arms folded in front of him.

What did *Dad* know? He was *old*. He had a thick quiff of all-grey hair on his head. (Jake couldn't remember a time when it was any other colour, even when he was little.) He had thin, dark eyebrows that pinched together in the middle. And he wore square-edged designer glasses that might have been trendy back in the thirties but certainly weren't any more. Who wore glasses now anyway? Why didn't Dad just get his eyes lasered, like everyone else? He was *so* uncool-and-old-school.

The car glided from the ramp and slipped on to the main road. Dad flicked on the AutoDrive, and it merged seemlessly into the steady stream of traffic that whizzed by all around. Cars, buses and trams flowed smoothly along the wide, flat roads between the buildings. Overhead, long transparent cyclotubes made criss-crossing bridges between the rooftops. Jake squinted to see the bike-riders inside, pedalling from one green, grass-covered rooftop to the next.

Jake sighed dramatically. Then, when he got no response, he did it again more loudly. His dad looked up from the speed and ETA numbers blinking on the navigation screen before him and raised a quizzical eyebrow.

'Okaaay,' said Jake, rolling his eyes. 'You can help me with it. If you like.'

'Wow. What a gracious offer. How could I possibly refuse?'

'Oh, come *on*,' said Jake. 'You want me to beg? Fine. *Pleeeease*, Dad, will you help me with my *stupid* climate-change project?'

'Only if you stop calling it stupid.'

'OK, fine. Deal.'

Jake's dad smirked and chortled lightly to

himself. Then he took a breath, and his face became serious. He pointed a finger past Jake, gesturing towards an old-style engine-car, rolling noisily alongside them.

'You see that?' he said. 'When I was your age that was pretty much all there was to drive. Liquid-fuel cars, with big, noisy engines.'

'So?' said Jake, sounding unimpressed.

'So that was a big part of the problem. Millions of cars like that were releasing thousands of tonnes of carbon dioxide into the air every day – altering the atmosphere and the global climate. And by the time we got round to doing anything about it, the world was already changing around us.'

'But we *did* do something about it,' said Jake. 'We started making electric cars instead, didn't we? And now only old fogeys and poor people drive those noisy junk-heaps.'

'Jake,' said Dad, a warning in his tone, 'that's not very nice.'

'What? I'm right, aren't I?'

'As a matter of fact, no. It's much more complicated than that. Electric cars didn't suddenly arrive all at once. Right through the early twenty-first century we were still making cars with engines alongside those with electric motors. Some people just didn't *want* plug-in electric cars. In the early days, electric cars were very expensive to recharge. And before the intercity charging stations were built, the fact that you couldn't go more than a couple of hundred miles on one charge was a problem. So most people stuck with what they knew: engines rather than electric motors. And car-builders found new ways to fuel their engines instead.

'Take that one,' said Dad, pointing again at the aging car beside them. 'What do you think it runs on?'

'I dunno,' said Jake. 'Old-school, dirty petrol?'

'Grassoline,' replied Dad. 'Cellulosic ethanol, made from recycled plant waste. And that one?' he said, pointing to the car in front.

'I give up.'

'Biodiesel. An older form of eco-fuel, which that guy probably makes at home by fermenting his food scraps and garden waste in a backyard bioreactor.'

'Whoopee,' said Jake. 'Good for him.'

'It *is* good for him,' Dad continued, ignoring Jake's less-than-enthusiastic response, 'and it's

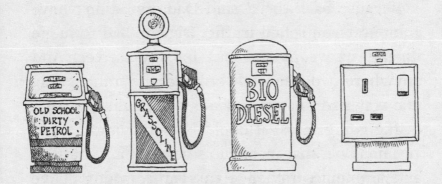

good for us too. It was low-carbon fuels like those that helped to wean us off petrol and clean up our cars.

'Plus, nowadays, lots of people choose not to drive cars at all. They just take the tram, or the bus.' He pointed to a speedy electric tram on their left side, fully loaded with passengers and zipping past the car traffic in its own BAT* lane.

'But wasn't it always like that?' asked Jake.

'No.' Dad laughed. 'It really wasn't. Trams only ran in a few big cities, and even then, you couldn't go very far on one. And buses and trams were so *slow* that you had to allow nearly an hour to get to work or school. And cars took even longer.'

'What?!' Jake spluttered. 'That's crazy! How could they be so slow?'

* Bus-and-Tram

'Because back then,' said Dad, 'we didn't have computer-controlled traffic. Drivers had to judge it, and weave in and out for themselves. And anywhere two fast roads crossed, the traffic going one way had to stop – at a big red light – so that traffic going across it could keep moving. As you can imagine, that meant lots of stopping, starting and jamming. On average, cars rarely made it above 30 miles an hour in big cities. And buses rarely got above twenty.'

As their car wove its way through another junction, Jake looked at the other vehicles as they slipped in and out of side roads. The cars, buses and trams flowed smoothly around each other like flocking birds. He tried to imagine it as his dad had described it – with stop lights and queuing at every junction. He couldn't. He gave up.

The car slid off the main road and up a long ramp to the railing station. There the AutoDrive guided it into position beneath the monorail, which stretched out across the city to the distant suburbs beyond. With a brief *whirr* and a sharp *thunk*, the roof-mounted drive wheels rose up to meet the rail and snapped firmly into position.

Within seconds, the car was cruising high over

roads and buildings, whizzing towards their destination at over 150mph. A little way off to the side, Jake could see a second elevated monorail, which ran parallel to theirs for a while, before curving off to the right. As he watched, a hovering Intercity MagLev* train suddenly appeared atop the rail. Within three seconds it was gone again – flying around the curve and out of sight, travelling at at least twice their speed.

* MAGnetic LEVitation

'What about the railways?' Jake wondered aloud. 'You had *those*, right?'

'Yes, we had railways,' replied his dad, already programming the AutoDrive to detach and rejoin the road at the next RADE* station. 'But believe me – they weren't *at all* like this.' Jake could see the station just up ahead.

The ElectroRailer slowed and the monorail dipped down as it approached the junction. (This was always Jake's favourite part of the journey – the sudden drop lifted his lunch into his chest, reminding him of the high-speed terror coasters at Chessington.) At the bottom of the dip, the roof wheels derailed in one swift movement, and the car dropped lightly on to the road, still rolling.

Before long they were home. As they turned into the driveway the garage door slid open to swallow the car. Jake picked up his pack and jumped out. Jake's dad emerged from the driver's side, leaned across to the wall, flicked the switch to activate the charging plate and closed the door. In the floor beneath the car, the plate buzzed and hummed as it recharged the battery.

'This is even bigger than I thought,' sighed Jake.

---

* RAiling-DErailing station. Where convertible car-trains attach and detach themselves from high-speed monorails.

'I'll never get this stup—' His dad frowned. Jake paused. ' . . . this *project* done by Friday.'

'Well, you've made a start,' said Dad. 'Perhaps your mum can help you with the next bit.'

'Great,' said Jake, and stalked sulkily into the house.

The Age of the Rechargeable Car

Imagine how different modern towns and cities would be if the rumble and roar of petrol-driven engines was replaced with the quiet whine of electric motors. What if millions of noisy, pollution-spewing cars, vans and lorries were removed from our roads and replaced by quiet, clean electric vehicles?

The nineteenth century was a time of coal, smog, steam trains and steam engines. The twentieth was an age of automobiles and aeroplanes – all driven by the roaring, climate-altering explosion of liquid fossil fuels. Could the twenty-first century finally be the age of cheap, clean, electric transport?

Oh, come off it. If electric cars are so great, why didn't someone invent one already?

They did. Over one hundred years ago. Round about the same time the first mass-produced petrol cars hit the road, in fact. Engineer Ferdinand Porsche (of later sports-car fame) built a prototype electric car with a motor in each of its four wheels. In the century that followed, a wide range of different designs were built. But beyond a few specialized uses (like milk floats), electric cars sadly failed to catch on as a twentieth-century invention.

OK . . . so why did they fail, then? Why aren't we all driving them now?

For a whole host of reasons. For starters, the huge battery arrays needed to power them were very heavy and quickly ran out. This meant most electric vehicles were sluggish, slow, inefficient and unable to travel more than 20 or 30 miles without recharging. That's fine for a milk round, but not much cop for longer trips and motorways.

But perhaps the main reason why electric cars failed was that they simply couldn't compete with petrol and diesel cars. With petrol being so cheap – at least compared with electricity – there was little reason for people to go for the few electric cars available, and little reason for big car companies to build more of them.

But now, a century after the electric car was first invented, all that is beginning to change.

Why now?

Because now we have new, improved materials from which to build strong, lightweight car bodies. We have new, improved technologies with which to build more powerful electric batteries and motors. And above all, we have new reasons to turn away from petrol: oil and petroleum are becoming more expensive, we have a new focus on fuel efficiency and cutting carbon emissions, and we have a new goal in protecting our planet's atmosphere. In this changed world of ours, replacing your pricey, dirty, petrol-driven car with a cheap, clean, electric one is starting to look like pretty *great* idea.

So what makes electric cars so much better than ordinary cars?

In short, they're quieter, cleaner and simpler.

Quieter, because there are no explosions going on inside an electric car, so all that's left is the gentle whirr of the motor and tyres.

Cleaner, because electric cars produce no exhaust fumes, and create just one-third of the carbon emissions of conventional cars. If charged with power from renewable sources – as it is hoped most will be in the future – they become even cleaner.

And *simpler* because – believe it or not – they actually have fewer mechanical moving parts, which makes them more reliable and easier to fix. Conventional cars have thousands of moving parts lying between the fuel tank, engine, gearbox, driveshaft and wheels. Electric cars have very few – a single, solid battery of lithium-ion cells (like thousands of rechargeable mobile phone batteries stuck together) electrically connected to one or more electric motors driving the wheels, and that's pretty much it. Solid computer circuits replace most of the gears, pumps and levers.

But what happens if the batteries run out?

Well, the car stops. Just like if you run out of petrol. But just as petrol cars have petrol gauges, electric cars have battery gauges, which warn you to replace or recharge the

batteries. Hopefully long before you trundle to a halt in the middle of nowhere.

So how do you recharge your ride? Can you just plug it in?

Basically, yes. You can recharge most electric cars simply by plugging them into a standard mains socket with a long cable! But a cleverer option is to plant an electromagnetic charging plate (in turn, hooked up to the mains supply) into the floor of your garage. Then you just park your car over the top of it, and the batteries recharge wirelessly, via a receiver pad mounted beneath the car. Recharging a flat battery like this can take as little as ten minutes, and a single charge will run the car for up to 250 miles.

Cool! When can I get one?

Right now, if you have the cash handy. The high-speed, all-electric Tesla Roadster sports car is already on sale in the UK and USA – yours for just £80,000. It has a top speed of 126mph, and recharges in just four hours. Celebrities like Arnold Schwarzenegger and Leonardo DiCaprio have already bought theirs.

If you want to go faster, how about the Shelby Aero Electric Vehicle? With a top speed of 208mph, and a recharge time of just ten minutes, it's the world's fastest electric sports car.

Stop it. I'm drooling . . .

Or maybe you'd prefer the British-made Lightning GT? That one has a super-lightweight, spaceship-sleek aluminium body and a computer-controlled electric motor in each wheel and is so quiet that it has a built-in 'engine-noise simulator' to warn terrified bike-riders and pedestrians of its speedy approach. Better still, you can adjust the engine noise heard *inside* the car so that it sounds like anything from a motorbike to a Formula 1 racing car.

That's it — I've gotta have one!

Yep, we've certainly come a long way from trundling milk floats. And the age of the electric car has only just begun . . .

Biofuels: Plant Power and Grassoline

What if the world's major fuels were not drilled from the depths of the Earth, but grown in forests, fields, parks and gardens? What if the dirty diesel and petrol burned in engines could be replaced with cleaner fuels recycled from grass clippings, waste paper or sawdust? And what if we could power our cars, buses, trams and trains, while scrubbing carbon from the air, regrowing forests and prairies and re-greening the world around us? Welcome to the wonderful world of biofuels ...

What?! Seriously? Cars and buses could really run on *plant juice*?

Absolutely. In a way, they already do.

They do?

Yep. And here's how ...

The petrol (or *gasoline*) that most cars run on comes

from the fossilized bodies of ancient plants (and animals). While they lived, they captured energy from the Sun and turned it into chemical energy within their bodies. After millions of years their energy-rich bodies – crushed deep beneath the ground or seabed – eventually turn into coal or oil. This we locate, promptly drill out and convert into energy-rich petroleum. So the stuff we pump and burn in our engines is actually a plant-based fuel, and our cars are already – in a sense – running on plant juice. A high-energy plant juice which, in turn, got its energy from the Sun.

OK . . . so what's the big deal about biofuels? What makes them so much better?

Biofuels are like cleaner, better petrol. They're plant juice: version 2.0. The end product is a type of fast-burning alcohol called ethanol, brewed using everything from corn and soybeans to weeds, waste paper and wood chips.

The big deal with biofuels is that – unlike fossil-derived fuels such as diesel and petroleum – they have the potential to be *carbon-neutral* fuels. This means that they trap at

BIOFUELS

CORN

SOYBEANS

WEEDS

PAPER

WOOD CHIPS

least as much carbon from the atmosphere as they release when you burn them.

So how do you make them? I'm guessing you don't just cram a bunch of weeds into your petrol tank . . .

No, not quite. Biofuels are made by harvesting (or recycling) plant material, transporting it to a processing plant and – typically – fermenting it in huge vats of yeast, which turn the energy-rich plant sugars inside into usable ethanol fuel. For sugar-rich crop plants like corn, soybeans and sugar cane, the process is fairly quick and simple. For tough, woody grasses and weeds it is a bit more difficult, as you first have to crack open their hardier cell walls to get at the plant sugars inside.

So what are we waiting for? Why don't we just start turning all that corn and sugar into motor-juice?

Well, many countries, including Indonesia, Brazil and the USA, have already tried – planting millions of acres of corn, soybeans and sugar cane for that very purpose. But as it turns out, growing edible crops to make biofuels seems to do more harm than good.

Why's that?

For starters, it's difficult to plant, grow, transport and process these crops without using more mechanical energy than you eventually get out of them as fuel. And because all the harvesters, trucks and other machines used to process the crops use fossil-based fuels, you also end up emitting more carbon than you save in producing the biofuel. Biofuel crops also displace crops used for real food, and it takes hundreds of litres of water and fertilizer to grow a single field of them. This causes local food and water shortages, along with groundwater pollution and soil damage. And worst of all, forests, prairies and grasslands are being cleared to make space for the biofuel crops, destroying natural plant and animal habitats and releasing stored carbon from the soil. All in all, not the best result.

Boo. So it's back to square one, then? We're stuck with our dirty gasoline?

Maybe not. Not if we work on making *grassoline* instead. Grassoline – or cellulosic ethanol fuel – comes from non-edible plants and plant wastes, including wild weeds and grasses, corn stalks dumped after harvesting, wood chips, sawdust from logging, waste wood and paper from paper making and even the thick green scum (or algae) that grows on the surface of polluted ponds. Producing these plants and plant products uses no extra land or water, and the energy used to recover and process them can be balanced out by the energy we (eventually) save in burning them.

That sounds good.

GRASSOLINE

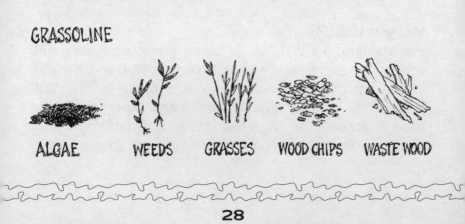

ALGAE   WEEDS   GRASSES   WOOD CHIPS   WASTE WOOD

But wait – there's more. These fuel plants don't just *cut down* on the amount of carbon emitted into the atmosphere by our vehicles. They can also actively *scrub* carbon from the air, undoing some of the damage already done by burning fossil fuels. As if that wasn't enough, they also remove pollutants from soil and groundwater, and provide natural habitats for insects and other animals.

We've a little way to go before the process is perfected, but one day you could be tipping your lawn clippings, waste paper – even your food scraps – into a dustbin-like bioreactor in the garden, and draining off clean, home-made biofuels to top up the tank of your car!

Superb! So I could be driving a rubbish-powered Porsche? Or a lawn-powered Lamborghini?

Probably more like a mulch-powered Mini, but who knows? Biofuels might never provide enough energy to meet *all* of our transport needs. But at the very least, biofuels like cellulosic ethanol, or grassoline, could help wean us off climate-damaging petroleum, and help us make the transition to even better renewable fuels in the future. And along the way, they could actually help re-green the world around us and restore the variety of plants and animals (or biodiversity) in ecosystems everywhere. Not too shabby, for a bunch of weedy rubbish.

Crowded Planes or Flying Trains?

Imagine a world where clean, safe, high-speed supertrains have all but replaced jet aeroplanes for long-distance travel. Every day and night, work commuters and holidaymakers flock to central terminals to board sleek tubular train coaches. As they speed between cities at over 300mph, passengers can stroll the spacious walkways, snooze in luxury seats, or enjoy non-stop movies, gaming and Internet access...

Oh, come on. Trains aren't really like that.
Actually, some are. And in the future, still more will be. In fact, for many long-distance journeys, trains like this could one day replace aeroplanes altogether.

Not likely, mate. Planes are *waaaay* better than trains. Everybody knows that.
OK... better, how?

Well, for starters, planes are faster. Much faster.

That's true. But high-speed trains are catching up.

Commercial airliners typically travel at between 300 and 500mph (500–800km/h). By comparison, most high-speed passenger trains currently operate at less than half that speed (120–220mph, or 200–350km/h). But in tests, high-speed supertrains in France, Germany and Japan have hit over 340mph (550km/h). And the technology is getting better all the time.

Plus it takes much longer to board a plane than a train. Because of the noise, airports usually sit far outside city centres, whereas train stations can be right in the middle of things. If you add up the time it takes travelling to and from airports – plus the longer waiting times at departure and arrival – you find that aeroplanes are rarely any faster than trains for journeys of under 600 miles (1,000km). In fact, in France, Spain and elsewhere in Europe, passengers are already abandoning planes in favour of trains for that very reason.

OK — but planes are still much cheaper. On the Internet you can get crazy cheap flights to Spain or Greece for, like, twenty quid . . .

Maybe, but not for long. As the world's coal and oil reserves run down – and become harder to find and extract – jet fuel will become more and more expensive. So unless we can find an alternative high-energy fuel, cheap air travel will soon be a thing of the past. Trains, on the other hand, could run on electricity supplied by cheap, renewable energy sources. Which would make them not only cheaper, but also much *cleaner* than aeroplanes.

Wait — future trains would be *cleaner* than planes?

Yep. In fact, even with the electric or diesel-electric engines of today's models, trains are *already* a far cleaner alternative to air travel when it comes to atmospheric pollution. It takes huge amounts of high-carbon jet fuel to get a 100-tonne airliner into the sky (and keep it there).

Over similar distances, trains emit up to 90% less CO_2 than planes, making their cost to the environment far lower. Since you don't have to get it airborne, you can fit up to twice the number of passengers on a train, which really helps bring down the amount of CO_2 emitted per passenger. And while jet planes are stuck with their jet-fuel addiction, future trains could become cleaner still – with the use of *clean electricity* from renewable sources, *biomass engines*, or even *zero-carbon fuels* like liquid hydrogen. All in all, a pretty clean ride.

But we already *have* aeroplanes and airports. Wouldn't it be really hard to change all that now?

Like I said, when the fuel prices and carbon emissions get high enough, flying will become so much more costly (to both our wallets and the planet) that we might not have much choice.

And in fact, we already *have* high-speed trains and railways too. In Japan, the Shinkansen (or 'Bullet Train') has been speeding between Japan's major cities for decades, while Europe's high-speed Eurostar has replaced many flights between London, Paris and Brussels. China has high-speed railways linking the cities of Beijing, Shanghai, Wuhan and Guangzhou, and is investing billions to build many more. And in the USA, plans are under way to link Los Angeles to San Francisco, and Chicago to St Louis using high-speed railways, replacing thousands of high-polluting airline flights each year.

OK, OK. So future trains could be faster, cheaper and cleaner. But there's no getting around it — planes are just *cooler*.

For now, maybe. But remember – the future of trains is wide open, and, believe me, there are some pretty amazing things now in the pipeline that might make you change your mind . . .

Like what?

How about a suspension train, which floats above its tracks and accelerates to incredible speeds using super-conducting electromagnets?

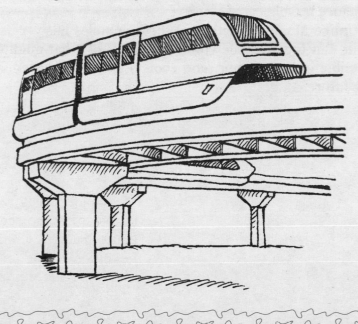

Magnetic Levitation (or *Maglev*) *trains* have been around for decades, and working Maglev lines already exist in Japan, China and Korea. While the technology is still in development, the incredibly high speeds reached by Maglevs (since the trains and tracks don't touch, there's little or no friction to slow them down) could eventually make them the future of high-speed rail.

Other ideas still in the works include the *AirTrain* and the *MonoMobile*.

The *AirTrain*, which looks like a cross between a spaceship and a roller coaster, hangs beneath its monorail track and accelerates with the assistance of four electric thrust fans, allowing it to tackle steeper gradients and curves than conventional or Maglev trains. The *MonoMobile* is a convertible car-train, which – like Jake's dad's car in the story – would run on roads over short distances but attach to an overhead monorail for high-speed, long-distance travel.

Unlike Maglevs, neither of these vehicles has yet been built. But together they offer a glimpse of what might be possible in the cleaner (and cooler) transport systems of the future.

Up in the Air

Picture yourself slicing through the air, 9,000 metres above the Atlantic Ocean, in a sleek, clean aircraft unlike anything you have ever seen. It is shaped like a huge triangular flying wing, powered by six high-efficiency jet engines and loaded with over 1,000 passengers and crew. Fifty miles out from its destination, the craft begins a steady, gradual descent towards an airport just a mile outside the city centre. On its final approach it glides – quiet and low – over roads and buildings, and touches down gently on the runway. Ladies and gentlemen . . . the aeroplane of the future has arrived.

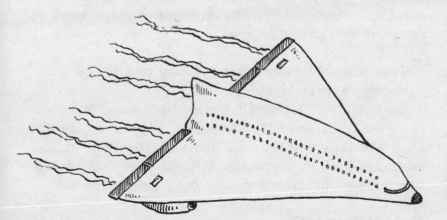

Hang on a minute. I thought aeroplanes were too dirty and dangerous for the future? Weren't we going to replace them all with supertrains and electric cars?

Some, perhaps, but not all. High-speed trains might one day replace aircraft for many types of journey. But speedy as they are, they still can't hop between the continents like an aeroplane. Even Magnetic Levitation trains need tracks. And it simply isn't feasible to build bridges and tunnels for spanning oceans like the Atlantic and Pacific.

OK, so what about boats and ships?

Yep – those are other options. Ferries and ocean liners can carry lots of people, and with clean, hydrogen-powered engines they could become a popular alternative to flying for many future globetrotters. But sadly, there's also a limit to how fast a hulking ship can safely (and efficiently) churn through the waves. And not everyone is happy with the idea of spending days or weeks at sea. Not if they have a business meeting tomorrow morning, or only a week to spare for their annual holiday.

What about hovercraft? They're pretty speedy, aren't they?

True, they are. Hovercraft ferries have been in action since the 1960s, and are still used for a few short, speedy channel crossings in Britain, Japan and elsewhere. In fact, engineers back in the sixties thought hovercraft would soon replace ships worldwide . . . but it never happened.

Boo. Why not?

Well, although hovercraft are faster, they're harder to

control and less versatile than conventional ships. The cushion of air they create (and float upon) decreases friction and allows speedy travel over calm, flat waters. But over choppier waters, and waves more than one metre high, they become difficult to steer and prone to flipping and sinking. And since one-metre waves are pretty common on the open ocean . . .

. . . you'd be in for a pretty scary ride?

Yes. To say the least.

For these and other reasons, hovercraft never quite made it off the ground as a world-conquering means of sea transport. So if we're going to keep making high-speed, ocean-spanning business and holiday trips in the future, we're going to need aircraft to do it. Cleaner, greener aircraft with all the speed (but less of the fuel-guzzling, air-polluting drawbacks) of today's jet airliners.

So how are we going to manage that?

One way might be by creating an alternative type of jet

fuel. Although it seems a little way off for now, it's hoped that hydrogen fuel cells might one day power aircraft using clean hydrogen fuel made from renewable sources. This would eliminate the hundreds of tonnes of carbon-dioxide gas that aircraft dump into the atmosphere with each journey. The only exhaust from a hydrogen-powered jet engine would be a cloud of water vapour.

Chemical engineers have also begun experimenting with making low-carbon jet fuel from fermented plant waste (just like the 'grassoline' we heard about on page 28). One group has even succeeded in flying a jumbo jet on a mixture of conventional jet fuel and an alcohol-based fuel made from fermented algae. Soon we could all be flying Algae Airways!

Ha! . . . or maybe Pond-Scum Pacific?

Could be!

Another way to make jet fuel better for the planet is to simply use *far less of it*. And that's where the cool, new, futuristic aircraft designs come in.

NASA and other aerospace companies are already experimenting with *blended-wing aircraft* like the one I described at the start of this section. In these 'flying-wing' designs, the body, seating and fuel tanks of the aircraft are built *inside* the thick double wings. This makes the whole aircraft more aerodynamic, which decreases the amount of fuel it uses on a long journey by 30–40%.

Combined with a new generation of *geared turbofan* engines that can power up and down more smoothly, these next-generation aircraft would be both cleaner and quieter than conventional, fixed-wing aeroplanes. And with quieter planes, you can build airports closer to city centres, allowing passengers to save on the fuel they would otherwise use getting to the airport and back.

So we'd all be jetting about in super-high-speed jet shuttles? Like something out of *Avatar*? That would be *brilliant*.

Maybe something like that, yes. But to meet the growing demand for trans-oceanic travel – especially from the increasingly wealthy populations of India and China – we'll probably have to go beyond just making aircraft sleeker and cleaner. We'll also have to make them *bigger*. That way, we can *decrease* the number of atmosphere-damaging *flights* required, by *increasing* the number of *passengers* each flight can carry.

Couldn't we do that with, like, giant airships or zeppelins instead?

Well, we *could*. And it's possible that long-distance airships might make a comeback in the future. But like ocean liners, airships are rather limited in speed. They're too bulky (so create too much drag) to be jet-propelled at high speeds. And being lighter than air, they're more at the mercy of high-altitude winds than aeroplanes. So what we'll really need is a new wave of redesigned, supersize airliners.

This new wave is, in fact, already arriving. The double-decker Airbus A380 'superjumbo' can carry over 800 passengers – almost double that of the airliners it was built to replace. Fully loaded, the A380 weighs over 650 tonnes, yet cruises at a speed of around 560mph (900km/h).

Yet enormous as the A380 is, even bigger aircraft are already being planned. One design – not yet built – is for a massive eight-engine 'saucer' craft, with a detachable passenger module in the centre. Imagine that – the plane would fly in, dump its detachable flight lounge on the ground, pick up another (perhaps with you in it) and be up in the air again within minutes. You could settle in for your in-flight movie at the airport lounge, and before the movie ended, the whole room around you would be speeding through the sky!

Wow! Talk about special effects!

Greener Paths and Smarter Traffic

Imagine a futuristic city designed for people rather than cars . . .

Wide, flat paths for walking and biking reach throughout the city, roaming everywhere cars can go and many places they can't.

Cyclists race between rooftops in see-through tubes that snake between buildings and loop over roads.

On the roads, buses and trams flow freely and quietly among the light car traffic, dropping passengers at office buildings and shopping districts.

Everywhere, people are taking greener, cleaner paths through the city. And the fresh, clear air shows no hint of its smoggy, car-clogged past.

Are buses and trams really that much better for the environment than cars?

For the most part, yes. Public transport vehicles like buses and trams can be loaded up with scores of people for each

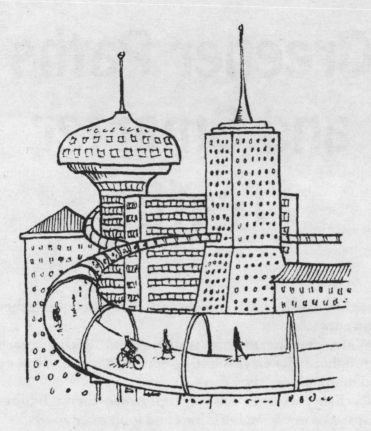

journey. Cars can only fit five to eight passengers, tops. That means public transport vehicles usually do far better than cars on the fuel used (and the air pollutants released) per person, and per mile travelled.

But don't they have bigger, dirtier engines than cars?

The old ones do. But in most modern cities, like London and New York, the old-style buses and trams are gradually being replaced with newer, cleaner models. Many have even started experimenting with hydrogen-powered buses on certain routes. These 'H-Buses' create no carbon emissions and release only water vapour from their exhausts. So along with helping to prevent climate change, they also stop the formation of smog in and around traffic-clogged cities.

It's hoped that in the future *all* public transport will be powered by either 'clean' electricity or hydrogen fuel, each produced from renewable energy sources like wind, wave or solar power (see the next chapter), rather than from fossil fuels. That way, millions of city dwellers worldwide will have truly clean, renewable ways of getting about each day.

Couldn't we just make all the cars H-powered and drive ourselves about instead of waiting for buses and stuff?

Well, that would be nice. But unfortunately – for now at least – there isn't much demand for 'H-cars'. And with very few of them on the roads, it's difficult to justify building hydrogen filling stations all over the place to refuel them. Buses, on the other hand, follow fixed, predictable routes and circuits. So you can just stick a single refuelling point at the central bus station, and each bus fills up with hydrogen when it returns. Simple.

Yeah, but would it really work? I mean, loads of cities have trams and buses. But millions of people still ignore them and drive everywhere anyway . . .

That's true. But that's because there's often no reason for people to ditch their cars and ride the bus or tram instead. If you already own a car, it's usually more expensive to buy bus or tram tickets than it is to burn a few miles' worth of petrol. Plus, on public transport, you have the added bonus of spending a whole journey standing up. Possibly with your nose stuck in someone's sweaty armpit.

Ugh. Why would you leave your car for that?

Exactly. But all that could change in the future. Oil and petrol will become more expensive as they become harder to find and process. And governments will probably increase petrol taxes, road tolls and traffic costs (like London's famous Congestion Charge). Eventually this will make car travel so expensive that people will happily leap from their cars and on to the cleaner, cheaper buses and trams. Provided, of course, that the cities keep building, improving and running them.

Hold on — with loads of buses on the roads instead of cars, won't that just make all the traffic move more slowly?

Not necessarily. Along with changes to their transport systems, some cities are also redesigning their roads and traffic signals to help increase the flow of traffic. Buses and trams can be given their own lanes (often in between the car ones), while traffic lights and junctions can be linked together to create a *Liquid-Flow Traffic System*.

This is a city-wide network of computer-controlled road junctions and signals, built to allow cars and buses to flow non-stop – under, over and through junctions. By avoiding the stop-and-go of standard traffic lights, this would actually speed up journey times for buses, trams, and the cars flowing around them. So if you need to get

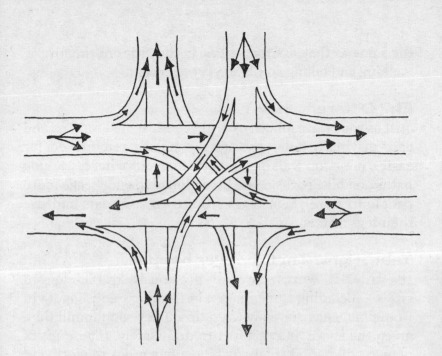

LIQUID-FLOW TRAFFIC SYSTEM

somewhere fast, you still can.

Besides that, not *everyone* wants to rush about as quickly as they can. Given the choice, many people might prefer a relaxing cruise to work on the bus or tram. Or if it's only a mile or two, perhaps a leisurely stroll or bike ride instead.

What, among all that non-stop traffic? You must be joking, mate. I'm not riding a bike into that lot. I can just imagine it: stop . . . look behind . . . signal to turn right . . . get arm knocked off by speeding bus . . .

Ah, but that's if bike lanes and walking routes stay roughly the same as they are today. But in the cities of the future, walking and biking could be very different.

Eh? Different, how?

Just as roads and junctions will be redesigned for free and easy driving, whole cityscapes could be remodelled for easier, non-stop walking and biking. Everywhere, walking paths and bike paths could be widened to encourage more people to prise themselves from their car seats and use their legs instead.

Yeah, right. That'd *never* happen.

It's true. It works. Several previously traffic-clogged cities – including Copenhagen in Denmark and Bogota in Columbia – have already tried this. They soon found that, given the space and comfort to do it safely, *thousands* of people will happily walk or bike a few miles to work and back rather than driving. And with thousands of kids walking or biking to school instead of getting dropped off, morning and evening traffic became much lighter, almost overnight.

Really?

Yep, really. And in the cities of the future it could all get better still. To make biking faster, safer and more fun, some engineers have suggested building elevated 'bike bridges' over and under city roads, and between the rooftops of some buildings. Built of tough, transparent plastics, these could connect streets, homes and shopping districts – allowing us to pedal safely around our cities without stopping for (or worrying about) road traffic.

Smart! We'd be like a bunch of happy hamsters, whizzing through our play tubes!
Err . . . yes. I guess you could look at it like that . . .

Only hamsters don't ride bikes. Obviously.
Right. Obviously.

Future Transport – Wordsearch

Hidden in the grid are twelve futuristic transport systems and fuels that we've already met in the book. How many can you find?

```
U Q K Q V I A K I D I Z W R A K W X M T L G
N Y G G Z Q E D S N D Z G M O D N H A E I L
I I R P Z B J L H G E U R O S T A R G S G L
D E A O Y N J Z E B F S M Z F N G A L L H G
Q N S R Y M T A L C I J N L F N T Y E A T N
K M S U T U P K B R T O M A T B T Q V R N X
P K O L V R B Q Y V I R D V K Q L I Q O I N
K B L K M G I L A U Y C I I K N S W H A N D
R N I E Q W X A E F K V D C E D I O D D G U
E X N O H M B U R M A B L B C S N H H S G C
O F E T O M O N O M O B I L E A E M S T T M
M C G E V V Z P E U C A W J J H R L M E L S
O K T W E A C G V W T N X I P J B B D R N U
F N I A R T D E E P S H G I H C L D Q O Z A
```

Airtrain
biodiesel
electric car
Eurostar

grassoline
high speed train
Lightning GT
Maglev

MonoMobile
Shelby Aero EV
shinkansen
Tesla Roadster

The answers are on page 215.

2. Future Energy

Monday night was football night for Jake's dad. So as Jake shuffled from the garage and into the living room, Dad disappeared upstairs to get changed. In thirty minutes' time, Dad would be running, chipping and shooting his way around the five-a-side court at the local sports centre with his mates, while Jake was stuck indoors with his stupid homework. Life just wasn't fair.

Jake's mum was a manager at the local energy company, but had been working part-time from home ever since his baby sister, Elise, was born last October. She was in the kitchen with her now, preparing for the messy chaos of dinnertime. But Jake ignored them both as he passed the high countertop that divided the kitchen from the living room. Without a word, he slumped into the big sofa before the TeleWall, flinging his backpack on to the seat beside him and his phone and keys on to the boxy glass table at his knees.

Inside the sofa, the Splashpower unit powered itself up and, after a quick bleep, began recharging the laptop inside his bag. A second later, the table answered with a bleep of its own, and a dim halo of white light appeared beneath his phone. As the phone began to recharge, camera images Jake had snapped earlier that day appeared in a circle on the flat digital table-screen. He fiddled with them for a bit – shuffling and zooming through them with light touches of his fingertips. But he soon got bored and turned on the telly instead.

'Hello, Mum,' said Jake's mum sarcastically. 'How was your day? Oh, it was lovely, Jake. Elise and I did your stinky washing and then we went to the park. Thanks for asking.'

'Hi, Mum,' said Jake, opening two TV windows on the digital wall and flicking through the channels. The wall buzzed and flickered into life, with high-definition 3D images of people chatting, arguing or sleeping appearing in each frame. Great, he thought. Nothing but stupid reality-TV programmes. He opened a third frame for email and scanned through his messages as he continued to flip channels in the other windows.

'So how was school?' said Mum, strapping Elise into her high chair. She wriggled and giggled excitedly, which meant this took a while to do.

'Rubbish, as usual,' answered Jake. 'We have to do this stupid project on the history of climate change – write about how everything's changed because of it.'

'Everything?' said Mum, done with the high-chair struggle, and making for the mashed-veggie baby food in the fridge. 'That sounds like a pretty big project.'

Jake sighed loudly – he was already bored with

channel-hopping and didn't want to repeat the whole story to his mum. He wished he could just fast-forward through the next ten minutes of his life. Or change the channel, and flick back when the boring bit was over.

'Like . . . transport, how we make and use energy, how we grow food, how we use water, how plant and animal life has adapted . . . all that stuff.'

'Well, I can help you with the energy, food and water bits,' said Mum. 'And maybe I can give you a lift to see Heath at the university tomorrow afternoon. He studies the effects of climate change on plants and animals, so he can answer your questions about those. Or if he can't, then he'll know someone who can.'

'Great,' said Jake glumly. This all sounded like *so* much work.

'Don't sound so enthusiastic,' said Mum, lifting a spoonful of orange slop to Elise's mouth. Elise giggled and swatted at the spoon with a small chubby hand. The slop catapulted off the spoon and on to Mum's forehead, which instantly doubled Elise's wriggle-and-giggle rate.

'Wa-hey!' said Jake flatly. 'Golly. Wow. I can't *wait* to start this thing. Really.'

'Look,' said Mum, wiping the goo from her brow with a damp cloth, 'you should count yourself lucky you have people willing to help. This *thing* will take you twice as long without me, Dad and your brother to chip in. Do you really want to spend days on end searching the Web instead?'

'No,' said Jake, frowning and sticking his bottom lip out. 'Of course not. The Web is way too big for that. I'd be on there for *ages*.'

'Well, then,' said Mum, 'if you want me to help, you can get off your lazy bum and help me with cleaning up the house. And with getting the shopping tomorrow. We can do it on the way to the university.'

'Oh, *Mum*,' moaned Jake, 'not the shopping. Anything but that. You *know* I hate it. Why can't you just order it online and have it delivered, like everyone else? Dave's mum does it.'

'Because it's expensive and wasteful. And besides, I like shopping for fresh food at the market. And if I have you to help me carry it back to the car, I don't need it delivered, do I? Now turn that thing off and come and load the dishwasher. We can talk about your project while you do it.'

Jake opened his mouth to argue, but then he

thought better of it. Instead he closed all the TeleWall windows, put down the remote control, and pushed himself off the sofa with a groan so ridiculously loud it sounded as if he was in pain. Shuffling into the kitchen, he picked up a few plates and started loading them into the high-speed dish steamer beneath the sink, sighing with each one.

Ignoring his complaints, Mum kept talking as she fed Elise, who by now was hungry enough to focus on her food.

'You kids today don't know how easy you have it,' she began. 'You have all the power and gadgets you could ever need, and you never have to stop to think about where it comes from, how it's made or what it's doing to the planet. But it wasn't always like that.'

'Seriously?' said Jake, with a smirk. 'You mean you didn't have electricity and computers when you were young?'

'Very funny, Jake. Your father and I aren't *that* old. No, we had electricity, all right. But for the most part we had to burn coal, oil or gas to produce it – all things that we knew were harming the environment and speeding up climate change. For a while it just kept on going that way.

'But pretty soon the demand for energy from growing populations – especially those in Asia and Africa – got so high that we could hardly meet it with coal and oil reserves alone. And this was right at the time when we wanted to be burning *less* of these fossil fuels – to protect our atmosphere and slow down climate change. Oh, and if you're done with those dishes, you can do the windows now.'

Jake flicked the button to start the dishwasher and grabbed a nanofibre cloth from the cupboard beside it. He gave it a quick rinse under the tap, then stretched up to wipe off the solar glass windows. The countertop was high, and he had to put one knee up on it to reach.

As he did so, he thought about the glass itself. All day long, he knew, the windows of the house were trapping energy from sunlight and turning it into electricity to power the lights and gadgets. It wasn't just the windows – the roof tiles and the paint on the walls were solar-electric too. And in the basement, a geothermal generator linked to pipes deep underground produced heat and electricity all day and all night. There were so many places to get free, clean power from. Jake couldn't imagine a world where they had almost run out.

'But why didn't you just use solar or geothermal energy instead, like we do now? Didn't people know how?'

'Yes, we knew how. But renewable energy sources like that weren't efficient enough to do the job back then. Before everyone had mini-generators, solar glass and Roofmills at home, we had to get all our energy from the main power grid. And that usually came from fossil-fuel power plants or from nuclear power stations. For many years we needed all our energy sources – including energy from cleaned-up coal and natural gas plants. Those – along with nuclear power – bought us the time we needed to develop solar, wind, geothermal and other cleaner power sources.

'And besides, you don't think *all* our home power comes from the solar-tech and geo-generator now, do you?'

'Errr . . . no,' lied Jake, 'of course not.' In truth, he did.

'Exactly,' said Mum. 'We get over half our power from the home generators, but the rest still comes from the grid, which is powered by a clean nuclear plant.'

'So what's the difference?'

'The big difference is in the way we *share* and *use* our power. In the old days, power was made at the power station and shared out to local grids and houses through transformers and cables. When we plugged something in and flicked the switch, it was like turning on a tap. The electricity was made in one place and used up in another.'

'And now?'

'Now the power travels both ways. We have a bi-directional power grid, where not just power stations, but also houses, office buildings and cars, can produce electricity. Each building has an energy *router* which *draws* power from the grid when we need it, but can also *return* power to the grid when we're making more energy than we're using.

'That way, not only do we use less energy all round, we also get paid for any extra energy we produce – energy that can be channelled to other houses and cars in the neighbourhood, so that we don't need to draw so much from the big nuclear power plant.'

Jake stopped rubbing at the windows, lost in thought for a second as he tried to imagine it all.

'Jake,' said Mum, 'if you're finished with those

windows, you can set the VacuBot next. I have to get Elise ready for her bath now. So if you could do that before you start your homework, that'd be a big help.'

Jake lobbed the cloth into the sink and strolled over to the beetle-like VacuBot sitting in its charging dock in the corner of the kitchen. About the same size as his backpack, this 'Bot was a new one that Mum hadn't yet got the hang of programming. Jake prodded three buttons, and the 'Bot surged into life, gliding from the charging dock and crossing the kitchen to the living-room carpet. With a whoosh, the vacuum function started and the 'Bot started tracing its programmed path across the floor. Jake followed it back into the living room .

Out of nowhere Austin, the family cat, appeared, as he always did when the VacuBot was operating. He circled it for a moment – judging its movement – and then pounced on top of it, perching himself there like a jockey as the 'Bot trundled and spun its way around the carpet.

This never failed to amuse Jake, and he regretted that he couldn't hang around to watch a bit longer. But it was time to start work on this stupid project.

Hefting his backpack from the chair – the laptop inside now fully charged – he grabbed his phone from the table and wandered upstairs to his bedroom.

Maybe, he thought, I could do, like, a couple of pages. Then I could open up a gaming window and see if Dave's online for a quick game of . . .

'And, Jaaaake . . . ' cried his mum from the bathroom, interrupting his thoughts, 'don't bother trying to log on to that World of Ninja-thingy game. I'm blocking it until you can show me that your project's done.'

Drat, thought Jake. She thinks of everything. I guess today was destined from the beginning to be totally fun-less. Hrrrrmph.

A Solar-powered Planet

Every living thing on Earth – from the tiniest bacterium to the tallest tree and the smartest mammal – depends on heat, light or energy from the Sun. Plants turn sunlight into energy-rich sugars, and animals eat plants (and each other) to obtain their second-hand solar energy. But what if we could harness the Sun's energy more directly? What if the walls and windows of your house could turn sunlight directly into electricity? And what if your car could run on liquid sunshine?

But that's so easy! Why didn't we think of that before?
How d'you mean?

I mean, we already *have* solar power, right? So why can't we just do all this stuff *right now*? A few solar panels about the place,

and ta-daa — problem sorted.

Well, unfortunately, it's not quite that easy. If it was – you're right – we probably would have done it already.

So what's the problem?

The problem is that solar power – as it is right now – is too inefficient and too expensive to supply all our power needs. The average solar panel converts less than 12% of the energy it receives from the Sun into usable electricity. The rest of the solar energy is reflected off the panel or lost as it heats up. So although sunshine is free, it's difficult to capture and convert enough of it to power something as large as an entire house.

Worse yet, the photovoltaic cells used to build solar panels are made from silicon – a valuable material which is expensive to purify. So, right now, solar power (or rather the solar cells and panels needed to harvest it) can't be produced cheaply enough to rival cheap, dirty fossil fuels like coal, gas or oil. The process of building solar panels also causes chemical pollution, and it uses up large amounts of water too.

Boo. Can't we just build better, cheaper ones?

Aha! Good idea. And in fact that's just what engineers across the globe are working on right now. Using super-thin layers of silicon, selenium and other materials, engineers are building a new generation of super-efficient solar cells. It's hoped that by 2050 these new, improved panels will be able to convert up to 30% of the sunlight that strikes them into electricity. This would make them almost as efficient as fossil fuels.

But wouldn't they still be expensive to make, with all that silicon and stuff?

A little expensive, yes. But we could save materials (and money) by building smaller panels, and using solar optics to concentrate sunlight on to them. Solar optics are dome-shaped glass or plastic lenses that sit on top of small solar panels to focus rays of light on to the cells beneath. This is just like using a magnifying glass to focus sunlight to frazzle an ant or burn a hole in a piece of paper. Only in this case, the light is converted into electricity rather than just heat. (And happily, no insects are harmed in the process.)

Unless they, like, crawl between the lens and the solar panel.

Errr . . . right. But then, arguably, it's their own stupid fault.

Hmmm. S'pose so.

We can also save on the amount of expensive metal we use in solar panels by spraying layers of metal molecules on to clear plastic sheets. This creates a cheap, flexible nano-panel which can be bent to fit the curved shape of a car roof or bonnet. In fact, several experimental solar-powered cars have already been built this way. And one of them won the annual World Solar Challenge race in Australia in 2009!

Niiiiice. I'd have one of those.

Wait – it gets better. Those nano-panels can also be built into clear glass or plastics to make *solar windows*, or mixed with ceramics and other materials to make *solar roof tiles* or *solar shingles*. Some chemical engineers are

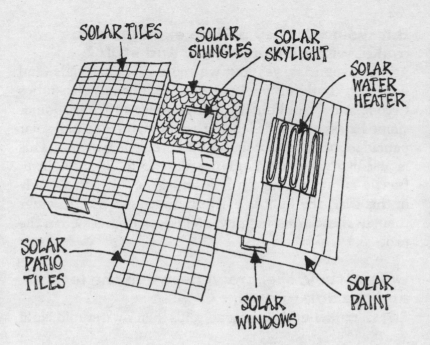

SOLAR TILES

SOLAR SHINGLES

SOLAR SKYLIGHT

SOLAR WATER HEATER

SOLAR PATIO TILES

SOLAR WINDOWS

SOLAR PAINT

even experimenting with creating *solar paints*. In these, sunlight-harvesting metals are mixed with plastics to make coloured liquid paints, which can then be slopped on to your house or car.

So instead of putting ugly flat solar panels all over your house or car . . .

. . . you might (some day) have them *built into* the roof and windows! Or painted on in flashy, hip colours!

Brilliant! Bring it on!

Hopefully we will. And soon.

So could you really power a whole house or

car like that? Just with solar paintwork and windows and stuff?

If advances in solar cell (and electric car) technology continue, then perhaps. The idea would be that the house or car would slowly charge itself as it sits in the sunshine, perhaps topped up by energy from the grid. But this probably wouldn't work equally well everywhere in the world.

Why's that?

Solar power works best, of course, in sunny climes. So it might work very well in the sunny parts of Africa, Australia, Asia, southern Europe and the Americas. In these places there's more than enough sunshine each day to charge batteries for use through the night. In colder, cloudier places – like Russia, Canada, New Zealand, northern Europe and the northern United States – there are far fewer days of sunshine per year, and fewer hours of useful sunshine per day. That means storing energy for days, weeks or months for later use, and lots of valuable energy is lost in the process.

So what could we do in the cloudy, rainy spots?

Right now there's no great solution. But one idea for the future is to find a way to convert sunlight directly into a chemical fuel rather than electricity. Liquid chemical fuels can be stored for long periods, and transported over large distances, without losing energy along the way. So chemical engineers are currently working hard to develop these 'liquid sunshine' fuels, along with the chemical solar cells needed to produce them.

We're still quite a way off many of these wonderful inventions. But if we succeed, we'll be one step closer to living in a truly solar-powered world – where cheap, clean energy from the Sun could be shining into homes and vehicles across the globe.

Hot Rocks and Poo Power

The Earth is a big, hot ball of rock, with a core temperature of 5,000–7,000°C, and a body made mostly of boiling molten rock. Just imagine if you could drill down and mine that raw energy to heat your house, create chemical fuels or produce electricity.

The Earth is also swarming with plants, animals and other living things. Plants live and grow by trapping energy from the Sun – energy which is transferred through food chains by the animals that eat them (and each other). As they live, die and decompose, most of this energy is lost as heat. But what if we used that energy to power our homes, our cars, our lives?

So let me get this straight — you want to use volcanoes and dead bodies to heat my house?

What? No! Well . . . not exactly.

Well, that's what you said. You said you wanted to drill a hole under my house to the core of the Earth. I'm not letting you do that. That's mental.

No, I didn't. Even if that was possible (which it currently isn't) or advisable (which it definitely isn't), you don't have to dig anywhere near that deep to harness the Earth's *geothermal energy*. In some cases, less than 15m will do the job.

What? You mean there's lava and magma bubbling away a few metres under my house? Yaaaghhhhhhhhhhhh!!! Run for it!!

Calm down. Unless you live right on a volcanic 'hot spot', there's no magma within 5,000–8,000m of your flooring. The Earth's crust is 5–8km thick and, with a few exceptions, the magma tends to stay happily under that.

Whew. That's a relief. Can I get off the table now?

Yes. You're fine. As I was saying – we're not drilling for magma, because you don't *need* magma to harness geothermal energy. You just need the heat that it transfers into drier rocks near the surface.

Almost everywhere on the planet, the upper 3m of the Earth's crust maintains a temperature of at least 10–16°C, heated by the Sun from above and the hot interior of the Earth from below. Beneath this lies a few miles of hot dry rock, shallower in some places than others.

Geothermal energy is produced by drilling deep wells into this dry rocky layer and channelling the heat to the surface. This is usually done by laying water-filled pipes beneath the ground, or by simply filling up the wells with water. Hot water returned to the surface can then be used to heat homes and greenhouses. Alternatively, it can also be used to create pressurized steam, which spins a turbine and generator to create electricity. And there you have it – clean heat and power from natural hot rocks. With no volcanic eruptions involved.

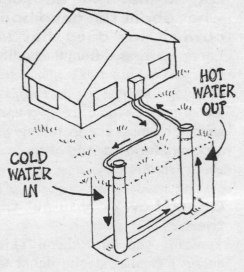

Oh. Well, that doesn't sound so bad. So could you do that anywhere In the world?

In principle, yes. But in practice the crust is thinner (and the rocks warmer) in some places than others. The ideal

GEOTHERMAL WELL

places are those found along cracks in the Earth's crust, known as *tectonic plate boundaries*. These spots include Iceland, Japan, the Philippines, New Zealand, Alaska and Hawaii. So, unsurprisingly, all these areas have at least one geothermal power plant in action.

What about elsewhere?

For now, at least, geothermal 'heat mining' like this is too difficult and expensive to do in places where the Earth's crust is thicker. But engineers are already experimenting with *low-temperature geothermal heat pumps and generators*. One day these might allow us to harness usable heat or electricity from the lukewarm 10–15°C layer of surface rock found almost everywhere on Earth.

OK. So that's the hot rocks sorted. But what about the dead bodies and poo power? How does that work?

Energy harnessed from the bodies of living things (and/or their poo) is known as *biomass energy*. You can use all kinds of living (or once-living) things to produce it, including wood, paper, whole trees, grasses, algae and food crops. In fact, biomass energy (along with hydroelectric power) accounts for over 90% of the world's current renewable energy resources.

OK, so how do you get the energy out of them?

Typically you burn them. This releases the chemical energy locked inside the plant body by transforming it into heat. This in turn can be used to boil water, spin turbines and generate electricity, just as coal, oil or gas-fired power stations do. But in some cases you can also use chemicals or enzymes to break up the starchy plant bodies, reducing them to high-energy sugars. These plant sugars can then be fermented or chemically cracked to make alcohol-based fuels for cars.

Hang on a minute — that doesn't sound very clever. Why would we want to burn through whole forests of trees and fields full of food crops just to make electricity and fuel?

Good point. We have, of course, been burning trees (and tree-derived fuels like charcoal) for fuel for thousands of years. But doing this on a huge scale – one large enough to support the modern lives of billions of people – solves one problem but creates another. Yes, we might have cleaner fuels for our homes and cars. But we'd also be destroying our environment and – if we're burning crops that could otherwise be eaten – our food supply. And that's *before* you consider the huge amount of carbon that forests remove from the atmosphere (more about that on page 163) or the huge quantities of water needed to grow crops. As a result, harvesting trees and edible plants for fuel, on a large scale, will not only fail to solve the climate-change problem – it will also leave the world starving, thirsty and treeless.

So what's the answer? What use is this biomass stuff if it does more harm than good?

The solution is to use *waste* biomass, rather than useful or edible biomass, to produce our energy. So instead of burning forests of fresh trees, we can burn wood chippings and sawdust from sawmills, recycled waste wood and paper. And instead of edible crops like corn or soybeans to create our energy, we can use inedible weeds, algae, crop stalks or other farm wastes.

Speaking of which – farms can also provide us with something even richer in energy than plant wastes: *animal* wastes. Chicken poop, pig manure, horse manure – all of these release energy-rich methane gas as they decompose. So by saving, processing and burning these poo products, we can add animals into the biomass mix, and use them to create (surprisingly clean) forms of poo power too!

Hmm. 'Waste not, want not', I suppose . . .

Exactly. If we're to switch to a clean-energy future, we can't afford to waste our resources any more. But if we dig

deep to harness the Earth's natural heat, and make better use of the wastes we create, then ours could be a better future – powered, bizarrely, by hot rocks, plants and poo.

The Wind and the Waves

Picture a bustling coastal city like Sydney, Barcelona or San Francisco – with skyscrapers, surf and warm sandy beaches. Now imagine if the sparkling lights of this city were powered not by coal, gas or nuclear power, but by the winds that breeze in from the ocean, or the waves and tides that wash its shores.

A little way off the coast, rows of clean, white wind turbines spin steadily in the fresh sea air, producing millions of watts of power per hour. Beneath the waves, huge tidal turbines turn silently and slowly, adding to the city's supply. Everywhere the natural flow of air and water is transformed

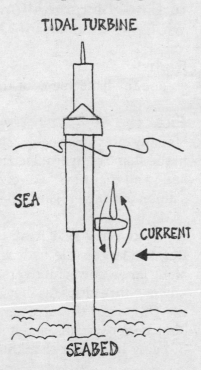

TIDAL TURBINE

SEA

CURRENT

SEABED

into a flow of safe, clean electricity. This is hydro-electrics for a new world.

Go on then. Tell me. I give up.
Tell you what?

How do you make electricity from waves and water? That all sounds a bit dodgy to me.
Why's that?

Well, electricity and water don't mix too well, do they? What if one of those sea-turbine things malfunctions? Won't it . . . ?
What? Frazzle all the fish?

Right!
. . . and the fishermen, for that matter . . .

Exactly!
Happily, no. We've been using water to produce electricity in the shape of hydroelectric dams for over a century now, and in all that time, we've yet to electrocute a river full of salmon (or anglers) anywhere.

Oh. So why not just use those then?
Because large-scale hydroelectric dams can only be built along large, powerful rivers. And while they can be used to power entire cities (as they do in parts of China, Brazil and the US), dams this size can also alter natural river flows, damage ecosystems, and flood entire villages in the course of being built. But thankfully there are less drastic ways

of harnessing water power. Namely, *tidal power* and *wave power*.

How are they any different?

Well, hydroelectric dams channel river flows into rows of tubes containing fan-like turbines. Each turbine is attached to an electric generator. As the turbine spins in the high-pressure water flow this machine produces an electric current.

Tidal turbines – which look like huge underwater windmills – contain electric generators too. But pushed and pulled by the surging tide, the large rotor blades of a tidal turbine turn much more slowly. A system of gears behind the rotor is used to transfer the motion to the generator further behind. From that point, an electric current is produced in the same way, and wired along submarine cables to a power station onshore.

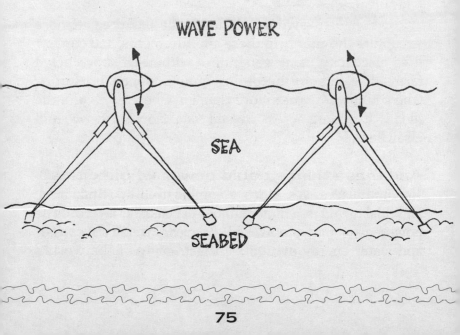

WAVE POWER

SEA

SEABED

Wow. Underwater tide-mills. Weird. What about the wave power?

Wave power is a bit different. It's produced from the wind-driven motion of surface waves. This is usually done using anchored chains of floating buoys (or 'ducks') which bob up and down with the swell. Inside the buoys, the bobbing motion is used to pump water (or a special hydraulic fluid) through a small turbine generator, producing electricity. From there, again, the electricity travels along undersea cables to the shore.

Electro-ducks. Even weirder. Does that really work?

Yes, it does. But as yet it's difficult to generate enough electricity this way to meet the demands of a whole city. Happily, though, most coastal towns are also whipped by steady coastal winds, which blow in from the sea by day and blow back out to sea by night. And this is where *wind power* comes in.

Rows of floating wind turbines can be anchored offshore to capture the energy in these air movements, and convert it to electricity using generators within. Offshore 'wind farms' like this are becoming quite common in Europe (the UK currently has more than anywhere else), and the idea is spreading across coastal Asia, North America and elsewhere.

And these things could power whole cities?

In some places, yes. With a combination of wind, wave and tidal turbines, a huge number of coastal cities could be powered (or partly powered) by clean, renewable wind-and-water energy by 2050. In fact, many of the world's

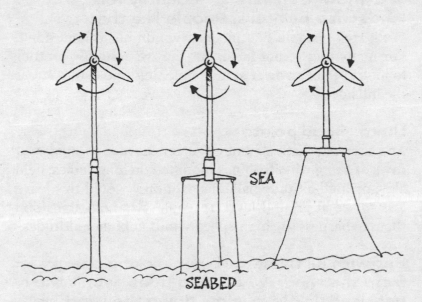

OFFSHORE WIND TURBINES

SEA

SEABED

largest cities – including Tokyo, New York, Shanghai and Sao Paolo – are coastal cities suited to this kind of set-up. Whether for fishing or trade, we humans have always depended on water to build our towns and cities. Now we're just using it in a different way.

But what about towns and cities that are inland, away from the water?

Well, some could still receive power from wind, wave and tidal stations based on the coast. Others might be too far away, but can still generate some of their power using land-based wind farms placed on windy hilltops, ridges and plateaux.

Won't that mess up the landscape? For,

you know . . . hikers . . . country folk . . . landscape painters. People like that.

Well, some people like modern windmills, others don't. For many they're not ideal, but they're certainly prettier to look at than a power station belching smoke out across the hillside.

Hmm. Good point.

And as an alternative, some engineers have even suggested rows of *flying* wind turbines mounted on long cables, held aloft by high-altitude balloons. Not only would this leave less to see at ground level, it would also better position them to harness the high-speed winds at higher altitudes.

But with all these turbines nicking energy from the wind, waves and tides, won't they get used up? Like, slow down the wind, or stop the tides or something?

Ahh, that's the beauty of it, you see. We *can't* use up the wind, waves or tides. The Sun provides the energy that heats the atmosphere to create wind and waves. And the gravitational pull of the Moon creates the tides. So while the Sun and Moon are still around, wind, wave and tidal power are truly limitless, renewable forms of energy.

For centuries, ancient peoples worshipped the Sun and Moon and imagined that they would bring power to their lives. Soon, through wind, wave and tidal power, it'll be as if the Sun and Moon are shining energy right into homes, cars and computers. And while they might form only one part of the solution to a clean-energy future, a world brightened *and* powered by the Sun and Moon is a pretty cool thing to think about . . .

Energy from Fossils and Atoms

Imagine a world where the prehistoric power of fossil fuels could be released without polluting the air and altering the Earth's atmosphere and climate. Where coal could be vaporized for cleaner burning, where gas could be burned beneath the ground to cut harmful emissions, and where the carbon released from burning oil could be pumped back into oil wells instead of released into the atmosphere. And imagine if nuclear power became a clean, safe and near-limitless source of energy for the future. If this all sounds pretty far-fetched, then think again – it might not be so far off at all . . .

What's so bad about fossil fuels and nuclear power anyway? I mean, I know they're not exactly *great* for the planet. But are they really that bad?

Well, yes and no.

The problem with fossil fuels – coal, oil and gas – is that

they take thousands (or even millions) of years to form, but only minutes to un-form.

Eh? How's that?

As you probably know, fossil fuels get their name from the process that creates them – fossilization. Coal, oil and natural gas are formed – over thousands of years – as the fossilized bodies of long-dead plants and animals are crushed beneath layers of sediment and rock. The energy packed into fossil fuels comes from energy-rich chemicals called hydrocarbons, which were formed and concentrated as the bodies were crushed and fossilized beneath the earth. So extracting and burning fossil fuels provides us with thousands of years' worth of stored energy.

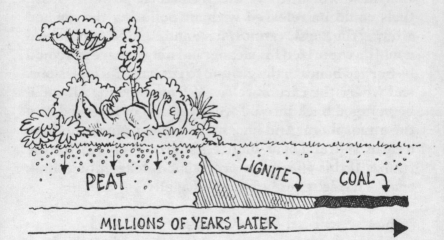

PEAT

LIGNITE

COAL

MILLIONS OF YEARS LATER

OK . . . but isn't that a good thing?

If you're trying to fuel a car, jet or power plant, then yes. But unfortunately, burning them also releases thousands of years' worth of stored carbon, in the form of carbon dioxide. As we learned in the intro, this is a greenhouse gas, which contributes to global warming when it is released into the atmosphere. Cue climate change, heatwaves, wildfires, drought, famine, melting ice caps, rising sea levels, storms, flooding, and so on.

Ah. Not a good thing, then.
No.

OK, so what about nuclear fuels? Do they release carbon dioxide too?
Actually, no. They don't Nuclear fuels release only heat (and other forms of radiation) as they are reacted to generate power. This heat is used to boil water into super-heated steam, which in turn drives turbines and generators to produce electricity. So that smoky stuff you see coming out of the huge cooling towers of nuclear power stations is actually just hot, clean steam, or water vapour. No carbon or other pollutants at all.

So people just don't like nuclear power because it can blow up and leak and stuff?
Pretty much, yes. In fact, nuclear plants are generally safer than coal- or gas-fired ones. Leaks at nuclear plants are very rare, and (nuclear) explosions are unheard of.

It *does* take a lot of energy (and water) to mine the uranium and other nuclear fuels, which contributes to climate change in itself. But the main problem with nuclear power is getting rid of *nuclear waste*. While it doesn't release gassy pollutants, nuclear-power production does leave behind solid radioactive waste materials. These wastes emit radiation that is hazardous to living things, and they might continue to do so for hundreds to thousands of years after they're removed from power stations.

OK . . . so if fossil fuels and nuclear power are so bad, why don't we get rid of them? Can't we just use clean, renewable things like solar and wind power instead?

That *would* be lovely. And that's certainly where we hope to get to one day. But, sadly, renewable power sources aren't yet ready to take over. They need much more development before they're able to meet the huge demand for energy in the modern world. Also, most countries* can't yet *afford* to ignore the cheaper, dirtier energy sources they already have.

By 2050, the world will probably be powered by a mixture of fossil fuels, nuclear power and renewable energy sources. Only later will we be able to drop fossil fuels altogether. So for now, at least, we *need* fossil fuels and nuclear power. But we also need to 'fix' them so that we can limit the damage they do to the planet.

How do we fix 'em?

For starters, we can use new technologies to burn them in cleaner, more efficient ways. Burning coal, for example, releases far fewer pollutants if you pulverize it into a black sandy powder, mix it with air and blast it into the furnace first. This is called 'coal gasification', and some coal-fired power plants are already doing it.

Natural gas can be burned more efficiently if it's done where it's found – deep beneath the ground. Engineers in Russia and elsewhere have been experimenting with

---

* China, for example, has billions of tonnes of coal buried within its borders, along with over a billion people demanding cheap energy to power their modern lives.

digging deep slanted wells into gas pockets beneath the Earth's surface, and then igniting them at the top of the well (a bit like lighting the wick on a big gassy candle buried in the ground) to produce a slow, controlled burn. Stick a power station full of generators on top, and bingo – instant energy.

But perhaps the most important fix is in capturing the carbon dioxide from burning oil, coal and gas and sticking it back underground before it can escape into the atmosphere. This is called *carbon sequestration*.

So how does that work?

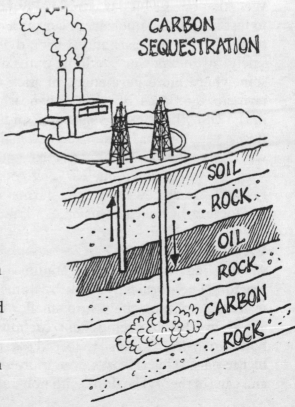

Basically, you put a gel-like plug inside a power station's smokestack, and bubble the waste gases from burning fuels through it. The gel material captures the carbon, which can then be released deep underground to be trapped in spongy porous rocks – perhaps in the very same oil well, gas pocket or coal mine the fuel was dug from in the first place.

So basically you're using the fuel, but sticking the carbon back where you got it from? Genius!

Exactly. The process is still being perfected, but if it works on a large scale, it could cut our carbon emissions from fossil fuels by 80% or more.

What about nuclear? How do we fix that?

Well, that one's a bit more tricky. For now, we might have to just keep using nuclear power (as a cleaner alternative to fossil fuels, at least) and storing the hazardous wastes safely at the power stations until we come up with somewhere more permanent to stick them. Many long-term storage places (like the one beneath Granite Mountain in the USA) have been suggested, and some partly built. But as yet, none has been used in a major way. Hopefully we'll figure this out within the next couple of decades.

In the meantime, nuclear engineers are continuing research into newer, better forms of nuclear-power production, like *nuclear fusion*.

What's that, then?

All existing nuclear power stations use *nuclear-fission* reactors. These basically crack the atoms within radioactive elements, splitting them into smaller ones and releasing energy in self-reinforcing *chain reactions*. In *nuclear fusion*, however, pairs of atoms are forced together and fused into bigger ones. This releases even more energy than fission, and can (in theory) be done with non-radioactive elements like hydrogen or helium.

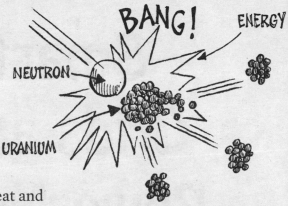

NUCLEAR FISSION

This fusion reaction, in fact, is pretty much exactly what happens inside the Sun, driven by the immense heat and pressure at its core. It's pretty much impossible to recreate those pressures and temperatures on Earth (at least, without using up more energy in doing so than you'd ever get out of the fusion reactor – which kind of defeats the point). So as we speak, engineers are trying to find ways to create powerful nuclear-fusion reactors (or 'mini-suns') at lower temperatures or pressures.

Some say it can't be done. (We've been trying for over 50 years, and no one's got anywhere with it yet.) Others say it can, and if they succeeded it could offer a clean (and almost limitless) power source that would probably solve the world's energy problems in one go!

Whoa. That would be something . . .

Here's hoping they do. But in the meantime, we can clean up our fossil fuels, take care with our nuclear fuels and work hard to switch over to renewable energy sources we already have – like solar, wind, biomass and geothermal power. That way, whether or not we ever manage to build mini-suns to power our planet, we'll still have saved it from the ravages of the Sun itself.

Smart Grids and PowerNets

Generating electricity is one thing. Getting it to where it's needed is another. For over a century, electric power has flowed from power plants, through power lines, to factories, homes and offices. And as cities worldwide grow larger, more plants are built to meet their growing demand for power.

But what if we could get by with fewer power plants, just by sharing the energy we already have? What if your home was smart enough to know how much energy it needed and could lend power to neighbours in an emergency? And what if it could produce its own energy, and sell extra electricity back to the power company, all by itself? Welcome to the PowerNet . . .

I don't get it. Why do we need a PowerNet? What's wrong with the electric grids we have?

Well, they're kind of outdated. And they're not very clever.

And they force us to generate more electricity than we
actually need.

Oh. Is that all?
That's just for starters. It gets worse.

The first electric power grids were built in the late 1800s
and, to be honest, they haven't really changed that much
since then.

In over 100 years?
Yep – pretty much. While the way we generate electricity
has changed a lot, the way we shift it about from place to
place has not.

A hundred years ago, almost all electricity came from
coal-burning power plants (with just a fraction coming
from hydroelectric dams, in the USA and elsewhere).
From the power plants, the electric current is transformed
and increased so that it can carry over long distances. Then
it's carried through high-voltage transmission lines (the
kind you see up high on poles and pylons) to local electric
substations, where more transformers decrease the
voltage to a safe, usable level. And finally, it travels through
more cables and wires to reach plug sockets in homes,
offices and other buildings.

OK. So what happens now?
Nowadays, we can produce electricity in many different
ways. We can use coal- or gas-fired power plants, oil-
burning generators, rows of solar panels, wind turbines
and more. But once the power has been produced, the
story is the same as it was a century ago. The electricity
flows, like water through a pipe, from power plant to plug

socket. At the far end, you switch the power on and off like a tap and the power floods into your lightbulbs, your TV, your laptop and your mobile-phone charger.

So what's the problem? It works, doesn't it? If it ain't broke, don't fix it, I always say.

Ahh, but it is broken. Or at least, it doesn't work as well as it could. The problem is that even if they're not using their lights, TV or laptop *right now*, everyone wants to be able to whenever they want. Think about it – you wouldn't be very happy if the power company only gave you light from 7 p.m. to 9 p.m. Or only let you use your laptop between the hours of four and six in the afternoon . . .

No way! That's just crazy!

That's what I thought. But unfortunately, this makes life very difficult for the power stations, as at certain 'peak' times (say, between 6 p.m. and 11 p.m.), almost everyone is using their lights, TV and other gadgets all at once. And even if they're not using them *right now*, they might want to *in a minute*. Which means the power companies have to fire up extra power stations (burning more coal, gas or whatever) *just in case* you need that extra power. At the very least, this wastes a lot of energy. Worse yet, if that energy comes from a conventional, fossil-fuel power plant, it also creates unnecessary gas emissions, which contribute unnecessarily to climate change.

Hmmm. That's no good. But what else *could* we do? I mean, besides switch off the TV, hum to yourself, and sit there in the

dark wishing you could read this book . . .

Good question. The answer is – we change everything, and create the power grid of the future: the PowerNet!

But how would that be any different?

Instead of working like water pipes – delivering water from a central reservoir to taps, in one direction – the new system would work more like the Internet. Information on the World Wide Web isn't stored in one central place and then piped out to computers across the planet. It's stored within all the memory banks of all the servers, PCs and laptops in the world. Internet routers and browser software (like FireFox or Internet Explorer) interact to send, request, or ping information between servers and computers worldwide.

Similarly, an electric 'Smart Grid' (or PowerNet) would share energy among all the homes, factories, power plants and other places where electricity is used, stored or produced. At each point, an *energy router* would manage the flow of power to and from the grid, just as Internet routers control the flow of information to and from the Internet.

But wouldn't the energy still just be flowing from the power plant to the houses?

Not necessarily. Not if some or all of the houses were generating their *own* electricity.

Houses with solar roofs and windows, roof-mounted wind turbines, biomass reactors or geothermal power generators (or perhaps a combination of these) might – at certain times – need to draw energy from the grid (and power stations) for power. When the sun goes down, or the wind drops, they have backup power from the grid.

But at other times they might be creating more energy than they can use or usefully store. With a Smart Grid, the energy routers could channel that energy to neighbouring houses, out through the grid to another town or right back to the local power station. Set up this way, groups of houses in a neighbourhood could compensate for each other if the power lines went down – like independent islands in a sea of power! Better still, the grid can use each and every house (and even, if they're plugged in, the batteries of electric cars sitting idle in the garage) to store excess power.

That way, electricity generated by power plants or houses during the day (when power usage is light) could be stored and shifted to where it was needed at evening peak times when usage is heaviest. In doing so, they could avoid having to fire up (or build) extra power stations to meet peak power demands.

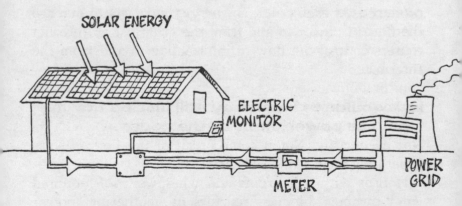

So it'd be like a big, friendly energy-swap?
Even better – a big, friendly energy sale. To keep the power-

sharing fair to those who produce power (rather than just use it), the grid and energy routers could keep track of *which houses* were donating and receiving energy, along with *how much of it* and *for how long*. So then the energy your house *produced* and *sent into* the grid would offset the energy it *drew out* and *used*. And your electricity bill would be a balance of those two numbers. If your house produced enough electricity, the power company could even end up paying you sometimes!

Right now, this is tough to do – as kitting out your house with things like solar panels, wind turbines and biomass reactors is very expensive. Plus the grid doesn't allow you to trade energy and get paid for it. But in the near future, the grid will be rebuilt smarter, and we'll be able to buy 'plug 'n' play' solar arrays, wind turbines and generators from DIY shops and install them ourselves!

Cool! Right — that's it. I'm building a super-green eco-house. It's gonna have windmills, and solar windows, and a poo-power unit, and . . .

Go for it! Start planning it now, and by the time you buy your first house, most of the stuff will be out there waiting for you. Then you'll be saving the planet just by sitting at home surfing the Net, video-gaming or watching TV!

Power and Energy – Quiz

Think you've got your energy sources sussed?
Answer A, B or C to each of the following questions, and
test the power of your knowledge. Or your knowledge of
power. Whatever. *The answers are on page 215.*

**1. Which parts of your house might one day turn
sunlight directly into electricity?**
a. Roof, walls and windows
b. Floors, doors and ceilings
c. Sinks and toilets

**2. Energy harnessed from hot rocks beneath the
ground is called . . .**
a. geographic energy
b. geothermal energy
c. thermolithic energy

**3. Which countries – situated on tectonic plate
boundaries – are ideal spots for hot-rock power?**
a. France, Germany and Italy
b. Zaire, Chad and Zimbabwe
c. Iceland, New Zealand and Japan

**4. Energy harnessed from the bodies of plants,
animals and other living things is called . . .**
a. biomass energy
b. biometric energy
c. poo power

5. Wave power is harnessed using . . .
a. ducks
b. seagulls
c. tide-mills

6. Tidal power is harnessed using . . .
a. windmills
b. tide-mills
c. sea-mills

7. Which of the following cities would NOT be a good spot for an offshore wind farm?
a. Sao Paolo
b. Shanghai
c. Salzburg

8. Fossil fuels include . . .
a. coal, oil and natural gas
b. coal, oil and nuclear
c. coal, nuclear and petrol

9. Nuclear power is made using which elements?
a. hydrogen and helium
b. uranium and plutonium
c. neon and krypton

10. Which energy source, if it worked, would solve all the world's energy problems at once?
a. nuclear fusion
b. nuclear fission
c. nuclear combustion

3. Food and Water

Jake was hot and sticky when he got home from school the next day. His V-shirt had done its best. On the walk back to Dad's car, the smart nanofibre material had expanded in response to his rising body temperature, spreading out the fibres and making itself airier and baggier. But it was no use. The sun was blazing, the air was muggy and Jake was soon covered in a thin sheen of sweat. And that just wouldn't do. Not when he'd be seeing Sarah in less than an hour.

Sarah was his big brother's new girlfriend. She had green eyes, pale perfect skin and long red hair that fanned out across her shoulders, like something off a shampoo advert. Yes, she was *Heath's* girlfriend. And yes, she was *ten years* older than Jake. But that didn't stop him being crazy about her. Or from stuttering and acting like an idiot

whenever Heath brought her around. Whatever, thought Jake. One day, she'll see that I'm the better guy. Unless, that is, she's repulsed by my zits and BO . . .

Holding that thought, Jake scrambled upstairs, pulling off his sweaty shirt and kicking off his trainers as he went. Grabbing a clean V-shirt and a clean-ish pair of jeans from his bedroom, he legged it to the bathroom, locked the auto-sliding door behind him, stumbled out of his dirty jeans and socks and leaped into the shower.

With a quick double-bleep, the sensors registered his presence and cool water sprayed down from a ring of small holes in the ceiling above. As Jake grabbed the body wash, a digital display set into the tiled wall ahead pinged on. It showed 00:01:59 in blinking red figures – the usual two-minute countdown beginning as he scrubbed furiously at his armpits. Won't be needing that today, thought Jake. And sure enough, 30 seconds of hurried scrubbing later, he was out of the shower and grabbing for a towel.

'Jaaaaaaaaaaake,' called his mum from downstairs, 'will you get a move on, please? I said I'd give you a lift, but I didn't say I'd wait around while you beautify yourself. You're only going to meet your brother, for goodness sake!'

It's not him I'm scrubbing up for, thought Jake. 'Commmmm-innnnng!' he yelled back, grabbing the ultrasonic-UV toothbrush, jamming it into his mouth and flipping up the toilet seat to take a simultaneous pee as he brushed. Nothing like a bit of multitasking, he thought.

With a flourish, he flushed the loo, spat in the sink, jammed his toothbrush back into its holder and yanked on his clean-ish jeans. The sink rinsed itself in a single quick burst, and the plughole gurgled as the water from the toilet, sink and shower mingled in the pipes below the floor.

Within a day, that water would be cleaned, filtered and sprinkled automatically on to the plants and flowers in the garden outside. But Jake wasn't thinking about that. He was too busy trying to find a matching pair of socks in his bedroom drawer . . .

'Jaaaaaaaaaake,' cried Mum, 'we're leaving now. I'm putting Elise in the car. If you're not here in two minutes, we're going without you.'

'OK, OK!' mumbled Jake, struggling to get the clean V-shirt over his head in mid-run. Reaching the top of the stairs, he scooped up his discarded trainers in one hand and bounded down the steps two at a time, almost twisting his ankle as he landed at the bottom.

From there, three more bounding strides took him out through the garage door, up to the passenger side of his mum's bubbly silver H-Wagon and in through the open door to the car seat. The door slammed shut behind him with a satisfying *thunk*.

'See?' said Jake, gasping for breath. 'Made it!'

Elise, in the back seat, giggled. Mum just rolled her eyes, and started the hydrogen-powered engine.

They arrived at the farmers' market ten minutes later. 'Grab the bags from the boot,' said Mum, as she transferred Elise from her booster seat to her buggy. 'Fruit and veggies here first. Then we'll head to the hypermarket for the rest.'

'I don't see why we can't just get everything at Best-Co's,' whined Jake, already jogging to catch up, a bundle of reusable shopping bags under one arm. He was always amazed at how fast his mother walked. It was like she had bionic legs or something.

'Because Best-Co's doesn't have locally grown fruit and veg,' said Mum. 'This way, we save on the energy used to transport them from farms abroad. Plus they're cheaper. And they taste better. Now stop dawdling and go and grab me a lettuce.'

Ten minutes later they were back in the car – the boot half-loaded with fresh fruit and vegetables and the AutoDrive weaving them through speeding traffic.

'I'm supposed to write in my project about how food has changed,' said Jake. 'Did you and Dad always shop like this? Did you eat the same sort of stuff back in the twenties?'

'Yes, and no,' said Mum, re-engaging the manual drive and turning off the motorway towards the hypermarket. 'Your father and I always shopped at farmers' markets, and the food there has stayed more or less the same. But these days farmers grow it very differently. They're not allowed to use chemical pesticides and fertilizers any more, and they use less than a tenth as much water on their crops.

'How did they manage that?' said Jake, fiddling with his still-damp hair.

'Once the water limits became law, they had to find more efficient ways of farming, and they had to give up some types of crop altogether. Farmers used to grow a lot more wheat, corn and rice, and the hypermarkets used to be full of processed foods made mostly of these and other grains. But now there just isn't enough land or water to grow grains and cereals on such a massive scale. So the farmers have changed the way they farm, and we've changed the way we eat.'

They pulled into the car park, and Jake grabbed a trolley while his mum saw to Elise. At the entrance, the hypermarket doors slid open before them, and Mum continued with her story as Jake scooted along beside her. Elise didn't like riding in the trolley's baby seat like other kids, preferring to be carried instead. This suited Jake, because then he was free to step up on the trolley and scull it along like an oversized skateboard.

'At one time, all these shelves would've been full of boxes of cereal and packets of biscuits, cookies and pasta. And over there, at the delicatessen, there were beefburgers, beef steaks, pork chops and packets of minced lamb. These days we don't eat nearly so much of that stuff, as it's all so expensive.'

'Because of the meat tax?'

'Partly, yes. When they realized how much water, energy and land it took to raise livestock for meat, the world's governments began taxing meaty foods. And now that the price of meat reflects the real cost of producing it, people don't eat nearly as much meat as they used to.'

'Didn't you have Synthi Steaks and Beetle Burgers back then?'

'Errr, no. We didn't. In fact, most people would've found the idea of eating algae and insects pretty revolting.'

'What?! Were they crazy?! I *love* Beetle Burgers! Especially with a bit of cheese and spicy sauce on top. Mmmmmm. Spicy Beetle Burger – I'm getting hungry just thinking about it.'

'Well, now we see things differently. To us, protein is protein. And with the new food-tech and designer flavours, we can make ground-up grubs, crickets and seaweed taste like beef, chicken or more or less anything we like. Only real snobs think they can taste the difference. And in proper tests, even *they* have to admit they can't.'

'What about seafood? Did you still eat that?'

'Yes, we did. But we generally ate more fish and less shellfish. After the ocean fish stocks started collapsing back in the thirties, most people couldn't afford things like cod and tuna any more. So they began switching to farmed shellfish, like oysters, mussels, clams, cockles and whelks.'

'Rightly so. I love a jar of whelks, me.'

'It's funny,' said Mum wistfully, 'my grandmother used to eat cockles and whelks all the time, but I never did when I was your age. And thousands of years ago, when the first humans travelled out of Africa, they moved along the coastlines, eating mostly shellfish as they went. In a way, everything has come around in a big circle, and we're back to where we started.'

This struck Jake for a moment, leaving him lost in thought and – unusually – without words for the rest of the shopping trip. He was still thinking about it when the car pulled off the motorway towards the university. But as they rolled up to the kerb before the main entrance, he quickly snapped out of it.

Heath was waiting there to meet him. And beside him Sarah stood smiling, her red hair fluttering in the breeze. They drew to a halt, and Jake checked his hair in the car mirror. *Disaster*. It looked like a bird's nest, and that zit was still glowing on his chin. Oh, well, he thought. Can't be helped now. He grabbed his bag and jumped out.

'Hey, bruv,' called Heath. 'How was shopping?'

'Fine,' Jake replied. 'Hey, Sarah,' he added, trying to sound casual and manly. His voice came out squeakier than he had hoped. Drat.

'Hi, Jake,' said Sarah. 'Nice to see you.'

Jake smiled at this. He was about to close the car door behind him when his mum leaned across and shouted, 'Jakey – you behave yourself now. And, Heath – have him back for tea. We're having strawberry choc ices – Jake's favourite. Bye, Honey-bun!'

Jake winced. Ouch, he thought. My pride.

'Will do, Mum,' said Heath, smirking. 'Come on, *Honey-bun*. Let's go.'

Hot, Crowded, and Hungry for Beetles!

Here's the bad news:

We're living in an unusually hot, crowded and hungry world, and as time goes on, it's only getting worse. Over the next century, average air temperatures will rise by 2°C or more, the world's population could increase to over 9 billion, and the starving and malnourished people could number over 2 billion.

But here's the good news:

While governments try to tackle the hot and crowded parts, we can tackle the hungry part ourselves, with smarter farming, smarter foods and perhaps some small changes to our daily eating habits. Bugburgers, anyone?

Whoa, whoa, whoa. What do you mean, hot, crowded and hungry? All right — I get that the world's warming up. But it's not that warm yet, is it? And, yeah, it can get a

bit crowded down the shops. But everyone seems like they've got plenty to eat where *I'm* from. A bit too much, some of 'em . . .

Well, that all depends on where you live. Chances are – if you're describing your hometown – you live somewhere in the wealthy developed world, where we tend to have very different ideas of what 'hot', 'crowded' and 'hungry' really mean.

What do you mean?

OK – here's what I'm talking about when I say *hot*.

On average, the world is warming up. With a few exceptions, air temperatures around the globe are rising. And in some parts of the world this is already having a fairly catastrophic effect on farming. Heatwaves, water shortages and extreme weather – made worse by climate change – are killing crop plants throughout Africa and south-east Asia. In a warming world, plants are being pushed past their natural temperature limits, and soils are being eroded and destroyed by floods and storm damage.

On top of all this, many of these same parts of the world are getting more and more *crowded*. By 2050, the world's population will have risen by around 3 billion people, with around half of that rise happening in Africa and south-east Asia alone. This, of course, will make the world even hotter, as more people farming, travelling and burning fuel will increase greenhouse-gas emissions, driving climate change even faster. But worse yet, it will also create more *demand* for food and water.

Now you don't have to be a genius at maths to figure out that: (less food available) + (more mouths to feed) = more hungry people.

And more hungry people means more *famine*, more *malnutrition* and more *fighting* (even warring) over the food and farmland that's left. In Africa, at least, we're already seeing this.

Ah, I see what you mean. But what can we really *do* about it?

Well, while governments are busy tackling the *heat* and the *overcrowding*,* we can at least have a go at tackling the *hungry*.

You mean rugby-tackle them and nick their food?! How is that going to help?!

Err . . . no. That would be no help at all. I meant 'tackle the *cause* of the hunger'. Not 'tackle the hungry people'.

Oh. All right, then — how are we going to do that?

Well, for starters, we need to take a good, hard look at the types of foods we eat each day, and what it takes to produce them.

In the developed world – and especially in Europe, Australia and North America – we tend to eat a very meaty diet. For most of history, humankind survived on nuts, roots, berries, vegetables, fish, shellfish and the occasional bit of meat from livestock or a trapped bird or animal. But with the growth of massive, factory-like cattle, pig and chicken farms, we now eat *waaaaay* more beef, pork and chicken than we used to.

---

* With, for example, new laws and agreements to help tackle climate change, and education and resettling programmes to address overpopulation – more about this later on.

What's wrong with that? I like beef, pork and chicken.

There's nothing wrong with enjoying a meaty diet. But the problem is that meaty diets are hard on the land and environment. Raising cows, in particular, requires huge amounts of grain and water, and acres of farmland just to graze them or grow their grain-feed. So if everyone in the world ate as much beef as the average American, Australian or European, we'd be out of water, food and farmland in less than a decade.*

So what's the solution? We stop eating beef?

Not necessarily. But if we're going to be realistic about feeding ourselves in a growing, warming world, we – in the wealthy, meaty developed world – might have to adjust the amounts of meat in our diets back to more reasonable levels. That could simply mean eating a little less beef and chicken, and a little more vegetables, beans, fish and shellfish.

* It would also accelerate climate change, thanks to cattle burps and farts! More about that on page 110.

Or . . . it could mean looking for protein from different sources altogether. Some scientists believe the alternative foods of the future might turn out to be fungi, algae and insects!

What?! Eat algae and insects?! Bleurgh!! No way!

Yes way! Think about it – if you eat mushrooms, you're already eating fungi. They're a good source of protein, and you can shape some types of fungi into burgers and steaks. Seen those Quorn burgers in the supermarket? Well, they're fungal protein, and believe me, they don't taste too bad.

Algal protein is much the same. You can grow it in huge vats, and shape it into a range of meat-or-chicken-mimicking forms. And since algae tend to grow well in warmer environments, they might just turn out to be the beef of the future!

As for insects, they're already being eaten as a delicacy in many parts of the world, including Africa, Asia and the Middle East. (See page 108 for some delicious insect recipes!)

Bleeurrghh! Stop it!

I'm serious! Who knows? In ten or twenty years' time kids might be happily tucking into McBeetle Burgers . . . or perhaps algae nuggets, with some crunchy crickets on the side . . .

Insect Recipes

Grasshopper Fritters
100g flour
1 tsp baking powder
1 tsp salt
3/4 cup milk
1 egg, slightly beaten
1 cup grasshoppers
500ml double, cream whipped until stiff
Oil for frying

Sift the flour, baking powder and salt together into a bowl. Slowly add the milk and mix until smooth. Add the egg and beat well. Pluck off the grasshopper wings and legs, heads optional. Dip the insects in the batter and deep-fry. Serve straight away, with salt to taste.

Popcorn Crunch
Here's an easy treat to prepare and take to the movies.
120g butter, melted
120g honey
3 litres popcorn, popped
1 cup dry-roasted insects, chopped

Blend the butter and honey together in a saucepan and heat gently. Mix the popcorn with the insects and pour the butter-honey mixture over it. Mix well. Spread on a cookie sheet in a thin layer. Bake at 350 °C for 10 to 15 minutes, or until crisp. Break into bite-sized pieces.

Cow Farts and Future Farming

There's more than one good reason for us to shift to a less beefy diet in the future. In short: *the meat we eat makes farts on farms*. The more livestock are bred and farmed worldwide, the more climate-changing greenhouse gases are released into the atmosphere.

Each year, rotting manure piles and belching, farting farm animals across the globe release millions of tonnes of methane and carbon dioxide into the air. And with the world's growing appetite for beefy burgers and meaty, western-style diets, by the year 2050 there could be millions more cattle making gassy contributions to the planet.

But with a few small changes to our diets and farming methods, we may yet avoid the perils of Global Guffing.

Wait a minute — you're telling me that farts could destroy the planet?!

No! Well . . . hopefully not. Not if we take steps to control the amount of greenhouse gases being guffed into the atmosphere.

But what makes cow farts so much worse than — say — human farts? I've got a mate who can do some pretty deadly ones. I bet *his* farts could destroy the atmosphere.

Granted, they might well destroy the happy, friendly atmosphere in your home or classroom. But even the most vicious and 'talented' human farters lack the equipment to damage the atmosphere on a *global* scale.

And besides – it's not so much animal *farts* that do the damage. More often, it's their rotting manure, or their belching and burping.

Fine. So it's rotting poo and burps, then. But what's so deadly about those?

In a word – methane. Methane is a gas released from rotting organic matter, like rotting plants, vegetables and animal bodies. But it's also released from rotting animal poo and from the guts of animals that eat tough grasses. These gassy, grass-eating animals are called ruminants, and include farm animals like cows, sheep and goats, and also wild animals like bison, wildebeest and yaks. This is why human farts aren't nearly as deadly. Because we can't eat (or rather, can't digest) grass, we don't produce anywhere near as much methane in our guts as ruminants do.

OK . . . so it's the methane that's bad for the atmosphere?

Right. Methane is a greenhouse gas – meaning it's one of

the gases that traps heat in the Earth's atmosphere – and compared to carbon dioxide (perhaps the most 'famous' greenhouse gas), it's around 25 times more powerful. That is, once released into the upper atmosphere, it traps and re-emits heat around 25 times more efficiently than carbon dioxide does.

Yikes. That doesn't sound good.

It's not. But thankfully, there isn't a great deal of it *in* the atmosphere. At least not yet. But the more livestock we breed for eating, the more methane is belched and farted, and the more rotting, methane spewing manure-piles are created.

Oh, come on — how much gas can a few sheep and cows really make?

You'd be surprised. A single cow can produce up to 110kg of methane per year. Stuffed into a big balloon, that lot would almost certainly outweigh *you*.

Wow! That's one big bag of burp!

. . . and that's just *one* cow. Now multiply that by the *1.2 billion* cows, sheep, goats and other ruminants on the planet, and it adds up to over *80 million tonnes* of methane released into the atmosphere every year. That's about the same weight as *1,000 aircraft carriers*. How's *that* for a windbag?

Blimey! But what can we do about it? I mean, we can't just off all the cows. They wouldn't be too happy with that solution.

No, they wouldn't. Nor would the millions of farmers who

depend on their livestock to make a living. But over time, we could at least help limit this meat-related methane damage by doing two things.

First, we can recycle the manure piles on farms rather than leaving them to rot and release their methane into the air. Done correctly, you can collect enough methane from harvested animal waste to power all the lighting and electricity of even a fairly large farm building.

Second, we could start encouraging farmers to produce more grains, beans or vegetables, rather than just breed huge herds of livestock. By gradually switching from a less meaty diet to one with more alternative sources of protein (see page 107), we can create more demand for veggies (algae, insects or whatever) while slowing the demand for meat. That way, we might at least be able to slow

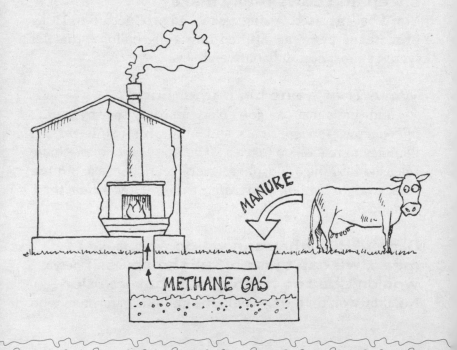

the growth of the huge factory farms that are currently supplying supermarkets with most of their cheap meat. Then less livestock will be bred, and less methane released.

But . . . but . . . then we'll have a planet full of vegetarians!

OK . . . and what's the problem with that?

Well, then the cow farts will be replaced with something even worse — vegetarian farts! I mean, have you ever smelt one? Urgh!

Hey – I said we could stop farts damaging the atmosphere, not stop people dropping stinky ones. That's another problem altogether . . .

Saving Our Clear Blue Treasure

Everybody knows that ours is a watery world. But few people realize that less than 1% of our blue planet's water is fresh and available for drinking. Freshwater supplies are already scarce in many parts of the world. And over the next 50 years climate change will most likely make this problem worse. Rising global temperatures will melt glaciers, create more storms and floods, and shift rains and snows. This will lead more fresh water to run uncaptured into the ocean – causing drought, famine and wars over the precious little that's left.

But what if we found new ways to save our clear blue treasure? What if we could capture fresh water from the skies and from the air around us? What if – in a changing world – we all took steps to make sure there was enough fresh water for all?

Hang on — less than 1% of the world's

water is drinkable? But the planet's *covered* with the stuff!

That's true, it is. But, unfortunately for us, over 97% of that is salty seawater, which is no good for drinking or for growing crops. Another 1% or so is frozen into the ice caps, or solid glaciers and icebergs. And a further 1% is too deep underground for us to get at easily. That leaves less than 1% of the world's water fresh, drinkable and available to the world's 6.7 billion people.

Oh. Now I get it.

Kind of makes you think, doesn't it? What's more, rising global temperatures and climate change could leave us with even less fresh water where we need it. While the warmer atmosphere will melt the polar and glacial ice – releasing it as fresh water – most of this meltwater will run straight into the sea before we can capture and use it. Plus warmer temperatures will lead to faster evaporation from rivers, streams and soils, leaving millions of people without clean water for drinking or watering their crops.

Add it all up, and this will mean drought, famine, war (over the remaining water sources) and disease (as people turn to drinking from dirty or polluted water sources) in many parts of the world. Not a very happy future for any of us.

But if we need water that badly, couldn't we just pull it out of the sea and take the salt out or something?

Yes, we could. Making fresh water from seawater is called *desalination*. And in some places we're already doing it. Some cities in Israel and Saudi Arabia make quite a bit of their fresh water by pushing seawater through special filters at high pressure, using powerful pumping machines. Other cities, like London, have started using this method to top up their freshwater supplies.

Great! Let's just do that, then.

. . . BUT – unfortunately – this process also uses tonnes of energy, so it's very difficult and expensive to make lots of fresh water this way. Even the few coastal cities that use desalination (like Tel Aviv in Israel) can't make nearly enough water to support their growing populations this way. And as for making *extra* for cities, towns and villages further inland – forget it.

OK . . . then can't we just dig deeper wells, and get more water from deep underground?

Yes, we can. We can, and we do. But if we go on like this, eventually there comes a point when the underground rivers and lakes (or *aquifers*) run dry.* In fact, this is already happening in many parts of the world.

Like in Africa?

Yes, for starters. But also in China, India, south-east Asia, South America, Central America, the south-western United States and even southern England. Cities in Bolivia, Peru and Mexico are already in trouble, and the number of water-stressed cities worldwide is growing with each passing year.

---

* Or, more often, when the underground water level in the soil (known as the *water table*) drops so low that you can't get at it without some *serious* drilling machines. Which of course most people – in most places – do not have.

Yikes. So what can we do about it?

Well, some countries are quickly realizing that if they can't keep looking below for more water, maybe they'll have more luck looking up . . .

You mean, like praying for rain? Or doing rain dances and stuff?

Not quite. More like harvesting rain, and capturing fresh water from the air around them.

How does that work? You just collect rain in a big tub or barrel in the garden or something?

Well, that's a good start. But some people are going a bit more high-tech. In California and parts of the south-western USA, homes are being built with complex *rainwater harvesting systems*, which capture and filter the hundreds of litres of water that fall on their rooftops every year. In these homes, rainwater runs from roof gutters into pipes and special storage tanks. There it's pumped (by solar-powered machines) through filters to remove insects

RAINWATER HARVESTING

WATER TANK

and pollutants, and finally pumped back into the house for drinking or bathing.

Smart! But if we can all do that, why would we need to 'capture water from the air' too?

Because in some places, like parts of South America and Africa, there isn't enough rainfall for this to be useful. Instead, some towns in Chile and South Africa are experimenting with fog-catchers – sail-like plastic membranes that are stretched out across plains and hilltops to catch and condense low-lying stratus clouds (otherwise known as mist or fog).

Just as gassy morning mists condense on to leaves to form watery dewdrops, water vapour from the air condenses on to these fog-catching sails and drips into collecting tubs beneath. Large fog-catching arrays can gather over 10,000 litres of water a day – enough to supply an entire village!

That's it, then! Water problem sorted, right?

Well, not quite. Even with all these clever water-harvesting technologies, we probably still won't be able to meet the world's thirst for water. Even if harvested rainwater and fog could provide enough fresh water for everyone to drink, there's no way we could capture enough to water all the world's fields and farms.

Around 70% of our fresh water is used for growing crops (mostly rice, wheat, maize and soybeans), so to keep feeding the world we'll also need to make much more efficient use of the water we have. That way, we'll not only be squeezing more water from the world around us – we'll also get more use out of each and every drop we collect.

Hmmmm. So how will we do that, then?

Glad you asked! We'll get to that next, so read on . . .

Drinking from Drains

The average European uses an average of *200 litres* of water each day for drinking, cooking, cleaning, bathing, washing clothes and flushing toilets. The average American goes through *600 litres* per day. Yet in sub-Saharan Africa, most people have to scrape by on *10 litres* or less. If we are ever going to even things out – and ensure that everyone, everywhere, has enough water to survive in our future world – then we need to do more than just save and collect more water. We need to find ways of *recycling* the water we're already using, and of decreasing the water 'footprint' of every household – to 50–100 litres per day, tops.

With the hydro-smart homes of the future, we might just manage that – by drinking, washing, and watering our gardens with water recycled from sinks, baths and even *toilets*! In a brave new world, we might have to be very brave indeed . . .

Drinking bath and toilet water??! UGH!! Why on *earth* would we ever want to do that?

Well, we might not *want* to, but there may come a point

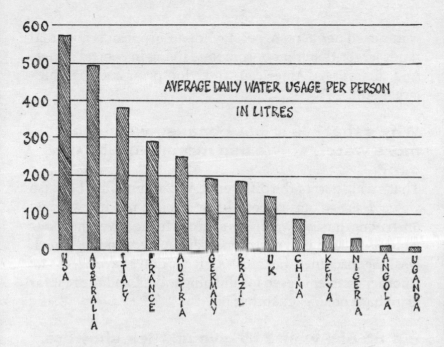

AVERAGE DAILY WATER USAGE PER PERSON IN LITRES

when we *have* to. If we want to reduce the water footprint of every home – especially modern homes in Europe and America, which use far more than their fair share – then we might not have a choice.

Hang on — what's a water footprint?

You've heard of carbon and energy footprints, right? Well, a water footprint is much the same thing, only it refers to the average amount of water we use (rather than the volume of carbon emissions we cause, or the amount of electricity and fuel we go through).

The average water footprint varies across the globe – as the amount of water you need to survive varies depending on climate, temperature and the way you live your life. But as a rough guide, the average water footprint (or amount of water used per person, per day) of a European is about 20 times larger than that of someone living in central Africa. And the average American water footprint is three times larger still!

Why's that? Is it just because we've got *more* water, so we use more because we *can*?

That's a big part of the difference, yes. But it's also because we've *designed* our modern lifestyles and machines based on having lots of water to spare. Hence, over half our water is used in large baths, power showers and high-tech washing machines that most Africans don't have access to. Another quarter is used for flushing toilets, and the rest for drinking, cooking and other uses.

But no one wants to give up their showers, washing machines and flushing toilets.

Right. And that's where water recycling comes in. Using clever filtering technologies, some homes in the drier parts of the western USA – like California and Arizona – are already recycling water from their kitchens, bathrooms and toilets and using it to clean their cars, water their gardens or even refill local drinking wells.

Ugh! But that's *disgusting*! And isn't it dangerous to drink toilet water? Not even my dog's allowed to do that . . .

Well, if you just lap it out of the toilet, then, yes – it's both disgusting and dangerous (so PLEASE don't try this at home!). But with proper treatment – with a specially designed water-recycling system – water from drains and sewers can actually come back cleaner and purer than normal tap water!

But besides that, very few systems actually return recycled water to the home for drinking, anyway. To stay on the safe side, most of them pump it out to the garden, or into a larger groundwater basin, where it mixes with fresh water from natural rivers and streams.

That still doesn't sound too appetizing to me. I wouldn't drink it. I mean, how do they *know* they've got all the poo and nasties out?

By carefully filtering, treating and testing it. Here's how it works:

There are basically two major types of water recycling – *grey-water* recycling and *black-water* recycling.

Grey water is the name given to used water that has been drained from showers, baths, washing machines and bathroom sinks. Basically, everything but sewage water from the kitchen sinks and toilets. Grey water might contain food residue, skin cells, dirt, crud, soap, detergent and a good number of microbes (bacteria and other microscopic organisms). But typically, none of this stuff is *that* nasty, nor is it *that* difficult to remove.

So in grey-water recycling systems, grey water drains from the household into a large storage tank – often buried underground, on one side of the house. From there it flows through a watery bed of reeds and gravel in a holding pond beside the house, which helpfully removes most of the larger pollutants. Next, the water is pumped through filters and chemically treated to remove the remaining nasties. And finally it's either pumped into sprinklers or irrigation pipes to water lawns and gardens, or returned to the house for use in clothes washing, cleaning or other non-drinking-water activities.

So what about the black-water systems?

Black water is the name given to the – ahem – somewhat dirtier sludge that drains from kitchens and flushing toilets into sewage pipes. Not only does black water *look* and *smell* worse than grey water, it also tends to contain far more dangerous microbes – nasty microscopic bugs capable of causing diseases if they get inside your body . . .

Yuck! See what I mean?

. . . so black water takes a lot more treatment during recycling before it can be made safe for re-use. Usually this is done on a large scale, at a specialized sewage-recycling plant outside the home.

Here, black water is chemically treated to kill microbes, then filtered through special sieving tubes and membranes. These membranes contain millions of tiny holes – holes so tiny that most microscopic microbes and viruses cannot pass through. And just in case any did get through, in the final stage, the water is zapped with UV radiation to finish 'em off.

At this stage, the water has become so pure that your normal tap water would look like muddy, gritty sludge by comparison. Now it's safe to inject it back into the local groundwater supply, to top up local lakes, wells and aquifers. Phew! Sorted!

Hmmm. I guess it doesn't sound that bad, when you put it like that. So does this really

work, then? Recycling can really save a lot of water?

Yep. Houses with grey-water recycling use up to 40% less water than those without. And black-water recycling can help replenish wells and aquifers many times faster than seasonal rains alone. It's hoped that in the future, recycling technology will become much better still.

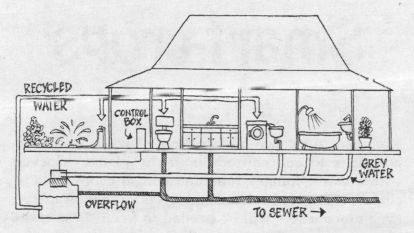

So good, in fact, that each home will have a self-contained water system that harvests and recycles grey water and black water back to the house – even for drinking – many times over before it finally has to be released into sewage pipes (and the sea). If that happens, we might be able to cut our water use to 10 litres a day or less. Which – in a warmer world – might come in very handy indeed . . .

Sponge-crops and Smart-crops

Each year over two billion litres of fresh water are bought, sold and shifted about the planet – locked within water-hungry food and cotton crops. And as climate change shifts rains and raises air temperatures, even more water will be needed to keep these trade crops growing.

The problem is, when water is shifted from one place, it's lost to another. And with precious little to go round, this could spell drought, famine and disaster for many developing countries in the future. Unless, of course, we found ways of growing food with less water, and of keeping more of the world's water where it's supposed to be . . .

I don't get it. What's the big deal about growing crops? People have to eat, don't they?

Of course they do. And growing crops for food and trade

isn't necessarily a *bad* thing to do. In fact, if we never did it, we could never have built our cities and civilizations. Without farming and trading crops, we could never feed and clothe more than a few hundred people at a time. We'd all still be hunting and gathering in small tribes, rather than living in cities, shopping at supermarkets, reading books and surfing the Internet.

There you go, then. What's the problem?

The problems come when you start using *lots of water* to grow *way more crops than you need*, so that you can *trade them for money* and *export them* to other countries. Do too much of *that*, and you'll disrupt the natural flow of water through your local environment. Add in the effects of climate change, and before you know it, you could end up starving, thirsty, broke and begging other countries to give your food and water back.

Wow. Could that really happen?

Yep. It can, and it does. And with climate change upon us, it will most likely become a lot more common worldwide.

But why?

It happens because exporting (or shifting) crops *globally* messes with the natural water cycle *locally*, with nasty effects over time.

Here's how it works.

In the natural cycle of water through the environment, rain falls from clouds (as *precipitation*) on to thirsty fields of rice, wheat, corn and soybeans. Well, either that, or it falls as rain or snow on to mountains, runs into lakes and rivers, and local people channel it to their crop fields and

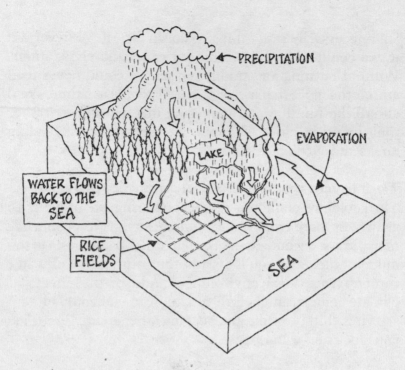

rice paddies using *irrigation* – but you get the idea.

Anyway, once absorbed into the soil, the water is taken in through the plants' roots, and helps the plants to grow.

Right. I get that much.

Now, while some water becomes locked in the watery cells of each plant's body, some runs out of the soil in underground channels and eventually finds its way back to the sea (where it will either sink and sit, or evaporate into the air again and form ocean clouds). The rest of the extra water inside the plants evaporates out of little pores in their leaves as gassy water vapour, in a process called *transpiration*. This process keeps plants cool, and is an important part of plant *photosynthesis*.

So now the water's back in the air again, and it rises up and condenses into clouds, which transport the fresh water back over land to the mountains and fields, and the whole cycle starts all over again. After a while, the crops are harvested and eaten, and everybody's happy.

OK . . .

So now let's go through the whole cycle again. But this time, imagine that the whole field is in a giant greenhouse, and that you've planted ten times as many crops as before.

Now you've got the same amount of water available as before, but ten times as many plants sucking it up. Worse still, as the air inside the greenhouse heats up more, the crops get thirstier, and you need more and more water to prevent them from drying out and dying. And at the end of it all, 90% of the precious, water-hungry harvest gets sold and shipped elsewhere.

These extra, due-for-export crop plants will soak up more and more of the available water in your area, meaning there's less available per plant, per field.

So what happens then?

Then the whole field dies. Not just the 90% of it you were hoping to sell, but also the 10% you were hoping to feed your family with.

Oh. I see. Not good.

It gets worse. If the soil gets hot and dry enough, it stops absorbing water altogether, even when it rains. Now you're left with fields of dusty, sandy or salty soil, useless for growing anything for years afterwards. If you're lucky, there's enough rain left to refill the streams and wells you get your drinking water from. If you're less lucky, even those dry up. Then you're in *real* trouble.

All that, from just a bit of extra crop farming?

. . . and a bit of climate change, yes.

So what can we do to stop it?

First of all, we take steps to combat climate change, so that the air temperatures don't get so high. Then we cut down on the 'sponge effect' by planting crops that require less water to grow.

In parts of Asia and Africa, where this is already happening, farmers can help to stop this by growing wheat, maize or sorghum instead of rice. If you've ever seen a waterlogged rice field (or rice paddy), you'll know that rice needs a lot of water to grow. Wheat and sorghum need far less, so can cut down on water loss in drier climates.

In places where soils have already begun drying out, we can take steps to protect the soil by planting trees as sheltering belts around the fields. These hold the soil structure together with their roots.

But what if the trees and wheat and maize crops won't grow because it's already too hot or dry?

That's where a little science can come in. Although there has been a lot of argument about Genetically Modified (or GM) crops, we've already developed GM crop plants that have been modified to survive on less water, that can tolerate higher temperatures and that can thrive in soils too salty and damaged for normal crop plants. It's hoped that in the future we'll be able to help countries suffering from the effects of climate change by supplying them with new seeds and plants more suited to the changing climate.

To do this, richer nations will probably have to get together and agree to help poorer ones (more about that in chapter 5). And this will probably also need to happen to tackle the main problem of those 'extra crops' causing 'virtual water loss' in poorer countries as they're sold to richer ones.

The only way to get round that will be to share farming technology and methods, and to make sure farmers in poorer countries get paid enough for their traded crops. That way, they won't have to grow so much, and will be able to afford to feed their families, make a living and keep their local water and environment safe.

That sounds fair enough to me.

Right. The world isn't always fair. But maybe the future world will be more so . . .

H₂0 – Quiz

How, where and when do we use our water? Who uses most, and how much? Ahh, questions, questions. Answer A, B or C to each of the following, and see how much you know about our planet's precious H₂0.

1. How much of the world's water is fresh and available for drinking?
a. 100%
b. 10%
c. 1%

2. How much of the world's fresh water is locked inside glaciers and icebergs?
a. 1%
b. 50%
c. 97%

3. How much fresh water can a fog-catcher nab?
a. 10 litres/day
b. 10,000 litres/day
c. 10,000,000 litres/day

4. Rainwater harvested from rooftops is filtered to remove ...
a. insects
b. viruses
c. stray cats

5. What is 70% of the world's fresh water used for?
a. growing crops
b. washing cars
c. flushing toilets

6. Water from toilets and kitchen sinks is called . . .
a. grey water
b. black water
c. brown water

7. How many litres of water does the average European use per day?
a. 2 litres
b. 20 litres
c. 200 litres

8. Based on average use, how many Africans could get by on the amount of water used by the average American in one day?
a. 3
b. 20
c. 60

9. In which dry, western American states are many people already recycling kitchen, bathroom and toilet water?
a. California and Arizona
b. Washington and Montana
c. Florida and New York

10. How much water is saved and re-used in a home with a grey-water recycling system?
a. 10%
b. 40%
c. 90%

The answers are on page 216.

4. Plants, Animals and Human Adaptation

Jake tried to act cool as he strolled through the university grounds with Heath and Sarah. Even standing as straight as he could, he was still two heads shorter than his lanky older brother. Nevertheless, he asked Heath lots of grown-up-sounding questions as they walked – hoping Sarah would notice – and tried hard to look unimpressed by everything around him.

This wasn't easy. The university was an impressive place – all shiny buildings, weaving cyclotubes and whizzing walkways. It was like an airport terminal with no ceiling.

'So,' said Jake, 'where *precisely* are we headed?'

'To my computer lab,' said Heath. 'You need to know about how the planet's changed for your science project, right? Well, that's the best place to show you.'

'And, err . . . what *precisely* do you study?' Jake had a vague idea that his brother did something with computers and geography, but had never bothered to ask him much about it before. He also thought 'precisely' was a very clever-sounding word, and was trying to drop it in wherever possible.

'I build computer models of global ecosystem–population change.'

'Right, right,' said Jake, nodding, though he had *no idea* what that meant. 'And what – *precisely* – is a global eco-sist?'

Sarah looked at Jake and raised a quizzical eyebrow. Hmmm. Perhaps he was overdoing it with the 'precisely'.

'It's not "eco-sist", cloth-head, it's "ecosystem". An ecosystem is the combination of the environment, the things that live in it and all the ways they interact with each other.'

Jake ignored the insult and stared straight ahead, avoiding Sarah's gaze. 'I see,' he said, furrowing his brow in what he hoped was a thoughtful expression.

'When something in the environment changes,' Heath went on, 'like the temperature, or the amount of food or water about, it changes how the living species survive and interact. I use computers to model the effects of climate change on human populations. Sarah studies the effects on plants, trees and animals.'

'Cool,' said Jake. He glanced at Sarah and grinned hopefully. 'I love animals.'

'You do?' said Sarah. She looked pleased. Jake saw his chance.

'Yeah. I've got two terrapins and a hamster. And I'm getting a tarantula soon.'

'No, you're not,' said Heath. Sarah turned to look at him. 'Mum won't let him have one,' he explained.

'Awwwww,' said Sarah, pushing out her bottom lip to make a jokey sad face and giving Jake a quick hug around the shoulders with one arm. 'Poor Jakey.'

Jake blushed. He was furious with his brother

for making him look like a little kid. But he was also overjoyed at Sarah's spontaneous mini-cuddle. He wondered whether to play it up for more sympathy and another hug. But then he thought better of it, and decided to act cool instead.

They walked on past the sports grounds, where students raced around the banked athletics track or played bionic hockey on the oval of solar grass within. As Jake watched, a player sprinted down the left wing with superhuman speed and chipped the ball high into the air above the goal. In the centre, a striker sprang five metres into the air to meet it, taking an overhead swipe with his flat-bladed paddle and smashing it down past the goalie at a blistering pace.

'Awesome!' squealed Jake. Heath and Sarah stopped in their tracks, surprised at his sudden outburst.

'Ahem,' said Jake, eyes cast down. 'I mean . . . this place is pretty cool.'

Sarah giggled.

'Come on,' said Heath, rolling his eyes. 'Let's go inside.'

Heath's lab was a wide room with a low ceiling, filled wall-to-wall with desks and computer terminals. It was surprisingly dark – the overhead lights kept low, Jake knew, so that the 3D holo-displays at each terminal could be clearly seen. A student sat at almost every desk, their faces lit by the flickering blue-green lights of the holograms before them.

Heath led Jake and Sarah to his own terminal, at the far side of the room. He grabbed two extra stools from an empty desk nearby, placed them either side of his own chair and sat down.

Immediately the display before him hummed into life, showing a glowing, blue-green globe in perfect 3D. The holographic Earth map rotated slowly as Jake and Sarah took their places beside him.

'Good morning, Heath', said a woman's low tones, apparently from somewhere inside the desk. 'Where to today?'

'Good morning, Kim,' said Heath. 'Show me forest cover and farmland, North, Central and

South America, time lapse: 2010–2050.'

'Understood,' answered Kim. Jake was impressed. Voice-input and integrated intelligence were standard in most computers these days. But these university computers were smarter than most, and Heath's sounded very posh. Like she went to Oxford or something.

The globe before them spun and zoomed to show a 3D map of the Americas. Beneath it, the date '2010' hovered in floating red digits. As they watched, the numbers flicked steadily upwards like a stopwatch, while floating patches of green and yellow appeared, shifted and disappeared in different areas of the 3D map above.

'What's happening?' said Jake. 'Are those all forests?'

'The green areas are forests, the yellow ones are farms,' said Heath, 'and this is what has happened to them over the last forty years. For the first ten or fifteen years, the forests kept shrinking and the farmland kept growing. Especially here in the Americas.'

'Was that because the warming air was killing the trees?' asked Jake.

'In the northern forests, yes,' answered Sarah,

'but in the southern hemisphere, it was mostly because we were still clearing forests to create new farmland. Up to this point, we were still chopping down an area of rainforest the size of ten bionic hockey fields every day.'

'Wow,' said Jake. 'It's amazing that there's any left at all.'

'But after this point,' said Heath, as the date below the globe ticked past 2025, 'things started to change. The global rainforest-conservation treaties kicked in, and developing countries began to get carbon credits for conserving and replanting their forests.'

Jake wasn't quite sure what that meant, but it sounded important, so he nodded thoughtfully once more. 'So . . . we saved the forests, then?'

'Sort of.' Sarah took over. 'But many forest landscapes had changed considerably, and many animal species couldn't stand the strain.'

Sarah paused and leaned towards the desk. 'Kim,' she said, 'new user –Sarah Wood.'

'Confirmed,' replied Kim. 'Hello, Sarah.' Voice-pattern recognition had long since replaced typed passwords for computer security.

'Hello. Now show us bird populations, time lapse:

2010–2050. Same zones.'

'Certainly,' replied Kim, and the coloured shapes on the map shifted once again. Countless small patches of red appeared and disappeared within the green forests as they shifted and shrank.

'In the Brazilian rainforests, many rare bird species were pushed to the brink of extinction by the destruction of their forest habitat. Some never recovered. There was trouble in Europe too,' Sarah continued.

With this, she reached up and touched the hologram with two outstretched fingers, spinning and slowing the globe as if it was a real object. The map stopped on Europe, showing small patches of red that flowed gradually northward.

'Here many bird species were unable to stand the summer heat, and migrated further and further north to escape it. A few species thrived in the newer, hotter Europe. But others disappeared altogether.'

'That's really sad,' said Jake. 'What about animals – how did they do?'

'Well, most lizards, snakes and other reptiles did fine, as did the frogs, newts and salamanders. Reptiles and amphibians tend to do well in warmer climates, and most were able to alter their behaviour to suit the changing environment. But some insects and mammals really suffered. Kim, show me Lepidoptera species, same zone, same time period.'

'Certainly,' said Kim, and the map began to shift once more.'

'Lepidoptera?' asked Jake.

'Moths and butterflies,' said Sarah. 'As you can see, many of them tried migrating northward to escape the heat too. But by 2040 many had run out of new places to go. Whole species flew out to sea, never to find land and never to return again.' The map images echoed Sarah's sad story, as small red patches drifted out into the sea north of Scotland and Ireland, and disappeared into the blue.

'And the mammals?' asked Jake. 'We saved the polar bears, didn't we?'

'Just barely,' answered Sarah.

Jake opened his mouth to make a joke – he thought 'just bear-ly' sounded pretty funny – but then he saw Sarah's serious expression and closed it again.

'But many smaller and less glamorous mammals, like voles and shrews, were pushed towards extinction too. Some of them didn't make it, while others had to move to new habitats, permanently, to survive.'

'Some of the bigger mammals did too,' added Heath. 'Like us. Some human populations had to be re-homed as their water supplies dried up and sea levels rose around them. Watch this. Kim – switch user. Me again. Show us global glaciers and ice caps, same time period. Go.'

The map zoomed out, showing the whole Earth once more. At the poles and throughout the world's largest mountain ranges, patches and lines of brilliant white light indicated the ice in glaciers and ice floes. As the date ticked onward, Jake watched as the polar ice shrank and little white lights were extinguished throughout Asia and the Americas. It was frightening how quickly some of them vanished.

'People never thought it would happen so fast,' said Heath. 'But once they shrank past a certain size, the melting of many glaciers accelerated, and within a decade or two they were gone. Whole villages and towns in the Andes and Himalayas had to be abandoned. And as the melting drove up sea levels – Kim, sea-levels, same period, please – many islands and holiday resorts were lost too.

'Look here,' he said, spinning the globe to show the Pacific Ocean. 'Past 2030 Tuvalu and other Pacific islands were flooding every year. Their people had to move to Australia and New Zealand to survive. And while the Maldives were never flooded completely, it was bad enough to drive away the tourists they depended on. Whole countries and nations, gone for good.'

'Wow,' said Jake. 'That's pretty heavy stuff.' He was starting to see now why his teachers and parents thought this project was so important. He had had no idea things had got that bad. By the time he was old enough to care about what was going on in the world, most of these things had either been dealt with or accepted. He felt guilty and slightly silly for moaning about it earlier.

'Is that enough for you?' asked Sarah.

'Er . . . yeah,' mumbled Jake, his mind still somewhere else. Possibly the Pacific islands. 'That should do it . . . I guess.'

'Better get you home, then,' said Heath, standing up. 'Thanks, Kim – goodbye.'

'Goodbye, Heath. Goodbye, Sarah,' said Kim. 'Have a nice evening.' The globe shimmered and vanished, and the computerized desk powered itself down.

'I have to drop my mate Tom off on the way home, so you'll have to sit with Sarah in the back. That cool with you?'

'Very cool,' said Jake, perking up once more.

Heath eyed him suspiciously. 'I bet.'

Sarah smiled, suppressing another giggle. Jake was glad it was dark in there so she wouldn't see him blush again

'C'mon, then,' said Heath. 'Let's go home.'

Living with Less Water

While politicians argue over whether climate change is happening, and countries quibble over what to do about it, people in many parts of the world are already dealing with its effects. Arctic sea ice is shrinking and thinning. Precious mountain glaciers are gradually melting away. And thousands are suffering from seasonal droughts made worse by a warming atmosphere.

From the desert dwellers of Syria and Iraq to the Inuit tribes of Canada, from the farms and vineyards of California to the mighty mountain cities of Bolivia and Peru – the proof of a changing world is there for all to see. For these people, and these places, climate change is not something they can choose not to 'believe in'. It's something they have to deal with every day. And something they'll have to adapt to, in order to survive.

Seriously? Is it really all happening *that* fast?

I'm afraid so. According to most of the world's expert climate scientists, the sea ice and glaciers of the Arctic, northern Canada and Siberia are thinning and shrinking

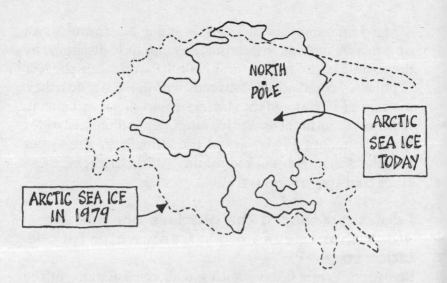

NORTH POLE

ARCTIC SEA ICE TODAY

ARCTIC SEA ICE IN 1979

year-on-year. If this continues, from the year 2030 onwards the sea ice in the Arctic could disappear entirely every summer. This could spell disaster for the many Inuit, Eskimo and other tribes who still live and hunt on the ice.

Why? Will they all fall in and drown or something?
No, but it will make living on the thinning ice a lot more dangerous, and many will lose their homes and hunting grounds. For some tribes, it could end their whole way of life – one they've enjoyed for thousands of years.

That doesn't seem very fair. And the mountains are melting too?
Yes. Well – not the mountains themselves, but the thousands of tonnes of fresh water locked into the ice on mountain *tops*, certainly.

Many mountain glaciers in Asia and in North and South America are melting so fast that they too could disappear by the middle of the twenty-first century. And while the loss of polar ice could affect *thousands* within the Arctic tribes, the loss of key mountain glaciers could affect *millions* in Asia and the Americas. Entire *cities* depend on meltwater from the mountain glaciers of the Himalayas, the Andes and the Sierra Nevada mountains. Without them, these cities could be in serious trouble.

I don't get that. If the glaciers are melting, won't that release *more* fresh water for the cities to use?

Sadly, no. While faster melting *does* release more of the fresh water locked in the glaciers, that doesn't mean the villages, towns or cities downstream will actually get to use it. As we mentioned in the last chapter, faster melting in the mountains often leads to more water running uncaptured to the sea.

If too much water is released at once, it cannot sink into the ground to refill wells and aquifers. Instead it runs quickly over ground in swollen rivers to the ocean – in volumes too great to be easily captured and stored by the towns and cities in between. Over time, the glacier simply melts away, and local people who have depended on the gradual, seasonal glacier melts for generations are left without enough water for their farms, homes and families.

And this is already happening?

Yes, it is. The *Ururashraju Glacier*, in the Cordillera Blanca mountains of Peru, is now less than *half* the size it was just 50 years ago. Over 300,000 people depend on it for fresh water, and local farmers and miners are already battling over the precious supply. By 2050 up to 77 million people in Peru, Bolivia and elsewhere in South America could face disastrous droughts as their mountain glaciers melt away. And while the Himalayan glaciers seem plentiful for now, up to a *billion* people in China and India could face drought by the end of the century if they continue melting at the current rate.

What about Europe and America? Will they have water trouble too?

Most parts of northern Europe, Russia and North America should do fine – for a while at least – as their plentiful lakes will be regularly refilled by rains shifting northward from the equator as the planet warms up. But the same shifting rains could spell disaster for places further south.

How's that?

Well, parts of the south-western USA, like California and Nevada, will be unable to support their huge populations (and their millions of acres of farmland) if the seasonal rains keep shifting northward.

And in southern Europe, shifting rainfall in the mountains of eastern Turkey could lead to a gradual drying up of the mighty Tigris and Euphrates rivers. They flow into Syria and Iraq, but if the rains keep shifting, and Turkey continues to dam these rivers off to save more water for its own farms and cities, it will almost certainly lead to drought and famine and 'water wars' in the Middle East.

Yikes. I didn't realize it was that bad. Is

there nothing we can do? Save the glaciers, or something?

For many of these mountain glaciers, it's already too late. So it's more about how all the different countries affected by water loss can work together to adapt to it.

Like how? By sharing water out fairly between countries?

That'll be part of it, yes. There will have to be international 'water summits', covering who *owns* the water, how much of it each country is entitled to *take* and how it can be shared out fairly without hurting any one country too much (more about this on page 208).

But it will also probably mean sharing *technology* and *ideas* between states and nations, so that everyone uses their water more efficiently and effectively. Many countries will probably begin to create laws limiting how much water each home, factory or farm can use. This will drive businesses and individuals to develop and use water-saving technologies, like the collecting and recycling systems we met on page 123.

So machines will come to the rescue, and solve the problem for us?

Maybe, or maybe not. Chances are that some things might simply have to go. In a future world, with strict limits on water use, the lush green golf courses of California and Saudi Arabia will be too costly to maintain. So they will either disappear altogether, or be replaced with artificial grass that needs no watering.

The same might go for large lawns and gardens in many of the world's biggest towns and cities – with hardly enough water to drink and recycle for washing, water might become too expensive for city dwellers to waste on thirsty gardens, even if they were allowed to. And if things get bad enough, some towns and cities might not survive at all. Desert cities like Las Vegas in the USA and Tel Aviv in Israel have only grown large because they have diverted (or piped in) huge amounts of water from rivers hundreds of miles away. In a world where water is precious and expensive, these and other places might one day have to be abandoned. (Either that, or they'll have to find ways of living on *far* less water.)

Wow. I doubt the people who live there will be happy about that . . .

Probably not. It could be that in a world with less fresh water available, people will become more selfish. States and nations will fight and squabble over supplies, spurring conflict, drought and disaster across much of the globe.

Or, perhaps people will *come together*. Perhaps we will all agree that *everyone* has the right to a fresh, clean water supply, and countries and governments will cooperate to make sure everyone has one.

Only time will tell, I guess . . .

World Population – Puzzle

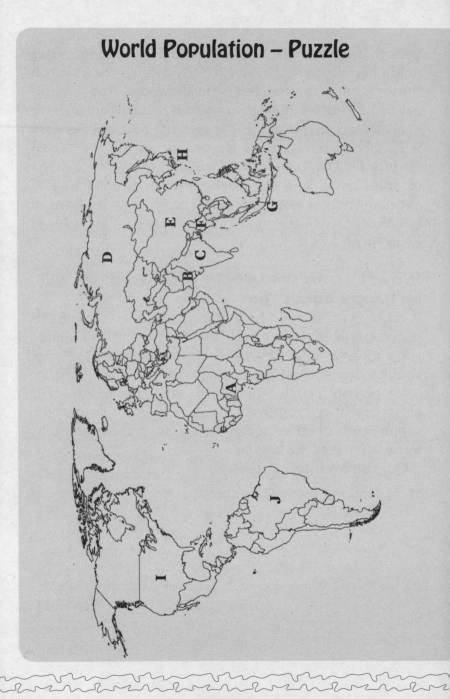

Ours is a crowded world, and by 2050 it'll be even more so. But do you know which countries have the largest populations today? Solve this puzzle and find out.

Match each country name with the correct letter on the map. Then try to match this country with its population and ranking (as of 2010) within the world's top 10 most populous places. The first one's been done for you: Nigeria is labelled 'A' on the map, and it has a population of 152 million people, making it the 8th largest country (in terms of population) in the world. Can you guess the others?

COUNTRY	LETTER	POPULATION & RANK (2010)
Nigeria	G	1.2 billion (2nd)
India	C	152 million (8th)
Indonesia	A	243 million (4th)
USA	J	184 million (6th)
China	D	310 million (3rd)
Brazil	I	156 million (7th)
Bangladesh	H	201 million (5th)
Russia	E	1.3 billion (1st)
Pakistan	B	139 million (9th)
Japan	F	127 million (10th)

The answers are on page 216.

Rising Tides

Despite what you might have seen in the movies, climate change is not going to flood our entire planet overnight. In fact, it never could, and never will. So there's no need to go building an ark or buying scuba gear just yet.

On the other hand, the world's ice caps and glaciers *are* slowly melting as the atmosphere warms. This is already raising sea levels worldwide, and the waters will continue to rise throughout the twenty-first century. Most of the world's towns, cities and nations will sit safe and dry above the waves. But for others, it is already too late. The damage is done, and the rising tides will be impossible to avoid.

So the world's not going to be totally flooded, then? Like in the Bible and stuff?

No, it's not. Even if all 30 million cubic kilometres of ice locked into the planet's ice caps and glaciers were to melt tomorrow, it would only raise global sea levels by around 60–70m. That would still leave most of the world's countries and land masses happily above water. It *would*, however, submerge large parts of Australia, northern Europe, south-east Asia and the south-eastern USA.

That doesn't sound good.

You're right. It doesn't. But thankfully there's no evidence that *all* the world's ice is going to melt any time soon.

On the other hand, some places in the world would be affected by a sea-level rise of just a metre or two. It's *these* places that are already being threatened by the creeping seas of the twenty-first century. And by 2050 some could be in *real* trouble.

You mean some places are already going under? Like where?

Well, nobody (or no place) has 'gone under' just yet. But there are quite a few regions worldwide that are already being threatened by rising sea levels. These regions fall into three main categories:

First up, there are the low-lying islands. In these places, the highest point on land is rarely more than a few metres above sea level. Which will pretty much doom them to a watery grave by the end of the century. These include the Maldives in the Indian Ocean, Tuvalu, Kiribati and the Carteret Islands in the Pacific, and Key West (just off the coast of mainland Florida) in the Atlantic.

Second, there are the regions that sit on low-lying coastlines, which will be severely affected by rising tides. These include parts of the Netherlands and south-east England.

Third, there are the places where people live on river deltas, or by saltwater rivers close to the ocean. These places include New Orleans, Bangladesh and large parts of Indonesia and the Philippines.

So what will happen to them? Will they just slip beneath the waves one day, never to be seen again?

In some cases, yes. Sadly this is *exactly* what will happen to some of the low-lying Pacific islands. But most of these places will be abandoned long before they are fully submerged, as regular, partial flooding makes them uninhabitable.

Couldn't they just put sandbags around their houses, and use boats to get about the place?

It's not quite as simple as that. Flooding does more than just fill streets and homes with water. It also brings with it drought, famine and disease – which can destroy a whole town or village even if the homes are left standing.

How's that?

When rising waves and saltwater rivers flood through a coastal town or village, the filthy, muddy saltwater often pollutes wells and aquifers. This leaves people without fresh water to drink, even while their homes are flooded.

When the same salty seawater floods coastal farmlands, it ruins the soil for decades, leaving it useless for growing crops. So even if the waters draw back, a devastating famine can follow.

And if sewage ponds or drains are flooded by surging waves in a coastal storm, it not only pollutes the remaining drinking water, but also spreads water-borne diseases such as typhoid, cholera and amoebic dysentery. So the flood scores a deadly hat-trick of drought, famine and disease, which makes it hard for a flooded town or village ever to recover.

Is there nothing we can do about it? We

just have to sit back and watch it all on the news?

Well, we can take steps to curb global warming and climate change, which might help slow the advancing waters. And in some places – like New Orleans, the Netherlands and south-east England – wealthy governments might be able to protect towns and cities with massive flood defences.

THAMES FLOOD BARRIER

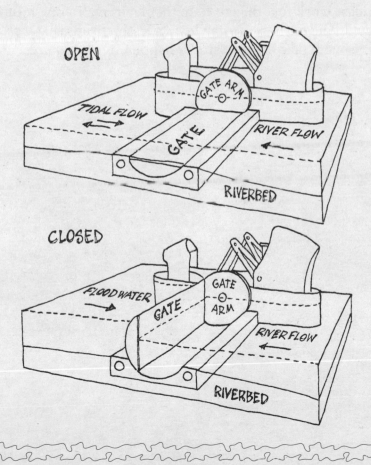

OPEN

TIDAL FLOW

GATE ARM

GATE

RIVER FLOW

RIVERBED

CLOSED

FLOOD WATER

GATE

GATE ARM

RIVER FLOW

RIVERBED

Large-scale water-pumping and reinforced sea walls and levees have saved these places more than once. And, for a while at least, they could do so again.

But for the poorer and less fortunate island nations, it might simply be too late. The best we can do is offer help and a new place to live. The government of New Zealand has offered the Tuvalu islanders a new home, for when they need it. Others are doing likewise for the people of Kiribati and the Maldives.

Even if we can't save the homes of these people, we can at least work together to help them survive in our future world. And perhaps we can learn a lesson from what we've done – and take steps to stop it happening elsewhere.

Glaciers – Anagrams

In which countries would you find these glaciers? The *glacier*, and its *mountain range*, are given on the left. All you have to do is unscramble the anagram clues on the right to reveal the *country* in which each glacier can (for now at least) be seen.

The first one's been done for you. Can you work out all the others?

Glacier	Range	Clue	Country
Ururashraju	Andes	RUPE	PERU
Athabasca	Rockies	ANA CAD	
Chacaltaya	Andes	VIA BOIL	
Siachen	Himalayas	AID IN	
Mer de Glace	Alps	RANCEF	
Aletsch	Alps	LARD NEWS ZIT	
Imja	Himalayas	PANEL	
Grinnell	Rockies	EDNA TEST SUIT	

The answers are on page 216.

Vital Forests and Vertical Farming

Everybody talks about 'saving the rainforest', but few people understand just how precious our planet's forests really are. Forests not only form hot spots of life and biodiversity, they also put the brakes on climate change – by pulling huge amounts of carbon dioxide from the atmosphere.

Now, as rising temperatures kill trees in Canada and Russia, thousands of acres of precious rainforest in Brazil and Indonesia are being logged for wood and paper or slashed and burned to create more farmland. If this continues, half the world's rainforest will be gone by 2025, and by 2060 there will be no rainforest left at all. And that will be bad news for all of us.

But with a few simple steps – and perhaps a few crazy new ideas – we can make wood and paper, build new farms, save the world's forests and put the brakes on climate change – all at the same time.

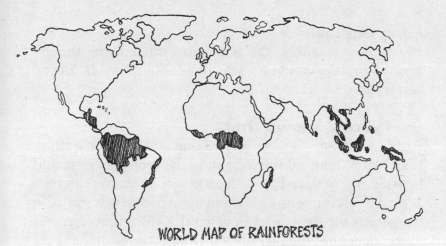

WORLD MAP OF RAINFORESTS

That sounds like a lot of work, just to save a few forests. Is it really worth it? I mean, it's not like we *live* in them any more.

Maybe *we* don't, but plenty of other creatures do. As we saw in the last section, forests are 'hot spots' for plant and animal life, and losing one means losing thousands of species to extinction. In fact, most of the world's biodiversity hot spots are forests. These include the famous tropical rainforests of Mexico, Brazil and Indonesia. But they also include cooler, temperate forests of Canada, Russia and northern Europe.

And while most of us no longer *live* in forests, we still depend upon them to survive. In fact, life – as we know it – could not survive *without* them.

Why's that? Do we need wood and paper *that* badly?

It's not the wood we need, it's the air. Or, more precisely, the atmosphere.

I don't get it.

Here's how it works. We (and most other living things) breathe in oxygen and breathe out carbon dioxide during respiration.

Everybody knows that.

Right. But if you think about it, if that was the whole story, then before long, all the oxygen in the atmosphere would be used up, replaced by a thick cloud of carbon dioxide. Which is, of course, toxic to humans at high levels, and also dangerous for the planet in general – since it accelerates climate change when it builds up in the atmosphere.

OK. But don't plants turn carbon dioxide back into oxygen again, when they do that photosynthesis thing?

Exactly. Trees and other plants help to control the amount of carbon-dioxide gas in the atmosphere by acting as a carbon trap or *carbon sink*. This – along with carbon-trapping in the sea and in photosynthesizing microbes – balances out the carbon from *carbon sources* (like breathing

animals, rotting poo and burning petrol), and keeps the atmosphere safe for all of us.

But that all depends on having millions and millions of trees about the place, in the shape of large forests, to trap all that carbon. And the trouble is, we've been steadily removing the carbon sinks (trees, entire forests) from the planet, while also steadily adding carbon sources (more people, more cars, more coal-, oil- and gas-fired power plants).

And in the last 50 years, especially, we've been doing both these things at a terrifying rate, and on a huge scale. We're using high-powered machines to clear forests in logging and farming. We're adding tens of millions more people to the planet every year. And we're burning more carbon-spewing fossil fuels than ever to power our vehicles and lifestyles.

But what else can we do? I mean, even if we do all that alternative energy stuff and stop using fossil fuel, we'll still need the wood and paper, we'll still want to have families and we'll still need the land for farming. So we can't stop.

Maybe we don't have to stop. Just slow down a little, and do things a little differently . . .

Like how?

For starters, we (or rather the world's rulers and governments) can agree to put limits on clearing forests, for the greater good of the world. That would only work, of course, if every country could afford to do it. Without all the money they would otherwise get from farming and selling wood and paper, it'd be hard to persuade poor farmers and loggers to stop chopping the trees down.

So we'd have to give them money? You mean, bribe them to stop chopping down the forests?

Not quite. First, we could encourage countries to protect their forests by offering them 'tree credits' for every acre of forest they save or replant. (Most countries borrow money from others to help their economy grow. So in exchange for the benefit they get from other people's forests, the *lending* countries could offer to let the *borrowers* off paying back part of the loan.)

Next, we could work to find alternatives to fresh-cut wood and paper, so that there is less demand for freshly chopped forest. That could mean producing and using more recycled paper – but then many of us already do this. Beyond that, we could use recycled wood chips and paper waste to create artificial 'recycled wood', for use in furniture or building materials.

But perhaps the most important problem to solve is the need for farmland. There's only so much land on the planet, and the more crowded the place gets, the more attractive the forest land looks to crop farmers and cattle ranchers.

So what do we do — build farms under the sea, or on the Moon or something?

That's one idea. But it's a bit drastic. A much simpler way would be to start farming vertically, instead of horizontally.

What?! What are you talking about?

I'm serious. If you think about it, we've been building our

homes upwards, instead of outwards, for quite a while now. At one time, everybody lived in single-storey huts or houses, on flat land. But now most of the world lives in multi-storey houses, flats and apartments. By the year 2050, over 80% of the world's population will be living in towns and cities. So if we already *live* and *work* vertically, why not *farm* vertically too?

How on earth would we do that?
By growing trees, crop plants and vegetables indoors, inside climate-controlled, glass-walled skyscrapers.

Like giant greenhouses?
Sort of, yes. Only they'd be specially designed to make use of the limited ground space in cities. Some would stand

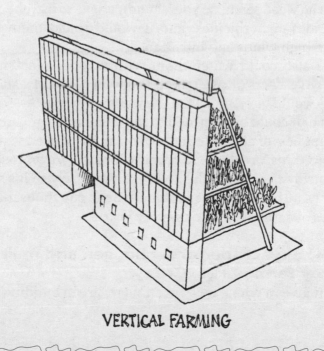

VERTICAL FARMING

on their own between office buildings and blocks of flats. Others might be built *into* them – with green 'farm floors' in and among floors of offices or living apartments!

Of course, we'd have to solve the problem of building and powering these vertical farm buildings without just creating more carbon emissions. (Hopefully we could build them from 'green' materials and power them with renewable energy sources.) But once that was sorted, there would actually be a lot of advantages to indoor, vertical, city-farming.

Like what?

You could control the temperature and climate more precisely, making it ideal for each growing food crop. The building would protect the crops from insects and airborne weed seeds, so you wouldn't have to use chemical pesticides or herbicides, and it would shield them from floods, high winds and hurricanes.

You also could water them with *recycled black water* from city sewers (as we talked about on page 124), and the plants would filter and clean the water as they grow, so that much of it could be returned to the water grid for use. And perhaps best of all, you cut down on all the fuel and energy used to *transport* the food from where it's *grown* (usually far outside the city, in the countryside) to where it's *eaten* (mostly in the city). This alone would cut thousands of tonnes of carbon emissions every year.

Wow! Skyscraper greenhouses and multi-storey farm-parks. Crazy.

Yep. It gives a whole new meaning to 'green building'!

Shifting Species

Animals and other organisms live in what biologists called *niches*. In part, an animal's niche is defined by where it lives, like a tropical rainforest, scorching desert or rocky mountain top. Through evolution, animals have adapted to habitats with certain temperature ranges and certain types of vegetation. But an animal's niche also includes its position in the food chain – what it hunts, and what it's hunted by. In the living world, everything has its place.

But now the climate is changing, and animal niches are changing along with it. Over the next 50 years many animals will try to move to new niches, travelling north or south to escape shifting temperatures and dangerous new predators. Where they succeed, we will see *migration*. Where they fail, we will see *extinction*.

But migration's not such a bad thing, is it? Don't lots of animals do it every year, anyway?

That's true – they do. Many animals, including birds, insects, whales and wildebeest, migrate to escape hot or cold weather, or to find new grazing, hunting and breeding grounds. But most of those animals only migrate *temporarily*. For the most part, they move back again as the seasons come around.

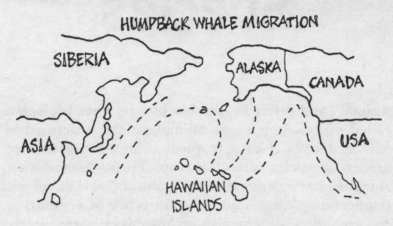

HUMPBACK WHALE MIGRATION

SIBERIA   ALASKA   CANADA

ASIA   USA

HAWAIIAN ISLANDS

NORTH PACIFIC OCEAN

So now some animals have stopped coming home?

In some species, yes. And over the next 50 years – as air and sea temperatures climb, more habitats are destroyed and more prey animals disappear – scientists think that more and more species will find themselves unable to return home to their original niche.

So what then? Where do they go?

Wherever they can. In Europe, many birds, beetles and butterflies are already shifting northward to avoid heatwaves and high temperatures in the Mediterranean region. And people in Canada are seeing, for the first time, many bird and butterfly species that previously only lived in Mexico and the United States.

So a few birds and bugs can't stand the heat and have to move north to find cooler homes. What's the big deal?

For some animals, it will be no big deal. They'll simply adapt and survive in their new homes. But for others, it will spell disaster.

How's that?

As we said before, new niches don't just involve new environments. They also come with new predators and prey. When a species is forced to move into a new area, it might be wiped out by predators (for insects – bats, birds and frogs; for birds – hawks, humans and egg-eating snakes) that it didn't have to worry about in its old niche.

Or worse yet, it adapts so well to its new niche that it becomes a *super-predator*. If this happens, it could wipe out entire species of prey animals it wasn't lucky enough to have around in its old home. (Picture a Great White Shark being dropped into a saltwater fish farm, and you'll have some idea of what I mean.)

Is that what you meant by 'migration and extinction'?

Partly, yes. Very few species will be pushed to extinction by rising temperatures and climate change *alone*. But when you add in the effects of dangerous new migrations like this – and of human hunting, fishing and habitat destruction – there are literally *thousands* of species that could be threatened with extinction by the end of the century.

Thousands? Wow. Which animals, and where?

Since it's hard to predict the long-term effects of climate change on animal habitats and food chains, we don't yet know for sure. But based on what we see happening already, we can take a guess at which species might suffer most.

In the world's oceans, the animals that build coral reefs are very sensitive to changes in sea temperature and acidity – both of which are already changing due to climate change. When the water gets too warm or acidic, corals become 'bleached', as the organisms that build them eject themselves from the reef, and either swim off or die.

. . . Which I'm guessing is bad news for Nemo?

Yep. By 2050, you might have trouble finding Nemo at all.

And it's not just the clownfish, but also the thousands of other reef fish, crabs, anemones and other species that depend on the coral for food and habitat. Over time, bleached coral becomes almost lifeless, as it's unable to support the rich variety of animals it did before. We're already seeing this in parts of Australia's Great Barrier Reef, and throughout the great Meso-American Reef off the coast of Mexico.

Elsewhere, in the northern Atlantic, the Mediterranean and the Baltic Sea, overfishing is already threatening hundreds of fish species. Some of these – like the Atlantic Cod, the Adriatic Salmon, the Baltic Sturgeon and the European Eel – could be pushed to extinction by warmer or more acidic waters.

What about on land?

There will most likely be extinctions there too. Especially among small mammals like bats and voles, but also some larger animals, like the European Mink and Eurasian Lynx. Even the humble European Ground Squirrel could find itself in trouble within a few decades.

But we can't let that happen! Can't we stop it?

Well, just as with the migrations of human islanders we saw on page 154, for some animal populations and habitats it might already be too late. In fact, some birds and mammals will suffer a worse fate than the people, as they'll be unable to move from their 'island' niches into new ones.

Some bird species live on only one or two islands in the whole world. Pushed out by warming temperatures or new competition, they might not be able to make it to another island (or the mainland) to find a new home.

And in the USA, small mountain mammals called Pikas live on virtual 'islands' of cool mountain tops. Unable to move *between* the mountain tops, Pikas are trying to shift further up the mountains to cooler climes. But many simply can't get high (or cool) enough. As a result, the Pika may be the first mammal species to be made extinct by climate change in the twenty-first century.

So the animals are all done for in the future? There's nothing we can do?

Well, they're not *all* done for. Some will do very well in the new, warmer world. Others will be lost to the changing climate. But for those in the middle, there *are* things we can do.

And that's what we're getting to next . . .

Looking After Life

We humans should count ourselves lucky. Our planet boasts a wonderful variety of living things. No one knows for sure how many different plants, animals, bacteria and other species there are in the world – some biologists have guessed that it could be over 100 million.

But now environmental destruction – made worse by the effects of climate change – is pushing thousands of species towards extinction, right across the globe. In our race to conquer the natural world, our vehicles, energy sources and lifestyles have been steadily destroying it.

But there is hope for the future. Over the last 50 years, conservation biologists have saved scores of species from extinction. If we make an effort *now* to protect the Earth's precious *biodiversity*, we could ensure a bright future for our world. Not just for ourselves, but for all the other living things with which we share the planet.

100 million?! Wow. Are there really *that* many living things on the planet?

Actually, there are at least *5 million trillion trillion* organisms (that's a 5 with forty-two 0s after it!) living on the Earth. There are over 6 billion of us alone, and there are *billions* of individual bacteria in every gram of soil. The 100 million refers to the estimated number of *different species* there are in the world.

As in, different types of animals and plants and stuff?

Exactly.

Whoa. That's even crazier. How do we know how many there are?

In short, we don't. There might be millions more, or millions fewer. But there are *1.5–1.8 million* species that biologists *already* know about. And from there, they can make an educated guess at how many – in each environment, and in each family of organisms – we can expect to find in future.

In reality, we might never discover them all, as some probably live in environments (like deep ocean trenches, or way down within the ice of the Antarctic) that are too difficult for biologists to explore fully. But together, these millions of species represent the total *biodiversity* (or variety of life) on our planet. And that's something we need to protect.

But if there are 100 million species kicking about the place, does it really matter if we lose a few here and there?

Good point. And in fact, there will always be extinctions, as new species are developing (through evolution) and old ones disappearing (through natural selection and extinction) all the time. But the problem is that thanks to us – and the habitat destruction and climate change we have wreaked upon the planet – species are now going extinct at 100 times (maybe even 1,000 times) the natural rate. So we're not just losing a *few*. We're losing a *lot*. And *fast*.

And even if you don't care about how rich with life your future world will be (which many people do), who knows what benefits those dying species could bring us if they lived? There might be plants lurking undiscovered in the rainforest that could cure cancer. Or chemicals in the blood of deep-ocean fish that could cure heart disease, asthma or diabetes. The point is, once they're gone, we'll never know.

But we can't save them all, can we?

No, probably not. Even if we all threw all the money and effort we have at the problem – which is unlikely – some of the damage is already done. The climate is changing, and entire forests have been reduced or destroyed. So we're bound to lose a good number of species, whatever happens.

So how do we decide which places and which species to protect?

Good question. That's no easy task. One way to do it might be to focus on special biodiversity 'hot spots' around the world.

How does that work, then?

Well, just because there are millions of species on the planet, that doesn't mean they're evenly spread out across its surface. Some places – like the Arctic, the Antarctic and the Gobi and Sahara deserts – are home to a fairly small number of species. Others – like the forests of Madagascar, the rainforests of Brazil and the heathlands of south-west Australia – are home to tens of thousands of species.

In total, biological 'hot spots' like these cover just 2% of the Earth's surface. Yet they contain almost half the world's living species. As if that wasn't enough, these are often also the places most under threat from climate change and habitat destruction. Around 70% of the world's endangered mammal species – plus 86% of its endangered birds, and 92% of its endangered frogs, newts and salamanders – live in hot spots like these.

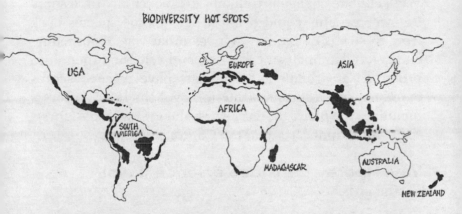

BIODIVERSITY HOT SPOTS

So we should protect these 'hot spots' over other places, because we'll save way more species for the future that way?

Right. If you only have a limited amount of money to go around (or a limited amount of land you can protect from farming, hunting and logging), then it makes sense to choose places you *know* will be worth protecting.

But that's not the end of the story. While protecting

hot spots might save the largest number of species, that doesn't mean there aren't species worth protecting outside of them. Nor that we should give up on species that are already close to extinction. The Arctic is certainly no biodiversity hot spot. But few people want to let the polar bears die as their icy homes and hunting grounds melt into the sea.

So could we, like, save pairs of nearly extinct animals until after climate change is over? Like Noah's ark, only without the flood?

Well, climate change is unlikely to be over any time soon. But we certainly could bring at least some species back from the brink of extinction in a similar way. By breeding endangered animals in captivity, and releasing them into protected environments, biologists have rescued scores of animal species from extinction over the last 50 years – including the Black-footed Ferret, the Przewalski's Horse, the White Rhinoceros and the California Condor.

Yay! Hooray for those science guys!
. . . and girls.

Right. Obviously. So if we do all that, we can save most species for the future?

Absolutely. Our future world could be one where national parks and nature reserves become Planetary Parks and Worldwide Biozones. With luck, we'll have the technology to keep our planet alive. But what's the point, if there's no life to share it with?

Endangered Animals – Wordsearch

All these animals are species that might be seriously threatened by the effects of climate change over the next century. How many can you find? Let's hope we can still find them in 50 years' time . . .

```
W C O R S I C A N H A R E P G G U T Y R R W
E U R O P E A N E E L N W N B F W R G F A K
S T Q A J G U H K H Z W G I Q D Q F H U E M
T G R O U N D S Q U I R R E L M N N M V B D
E U R A S I A N L Y N X I L L D E S M A N M
R R K T A B D E R A E G N O L S G U M M W Z
N A T L A N T I C C O D K B W E H O L Y O U
G K M T A C E L O P D E L B R A M A A K R D
E X A P O L L O B U T T E R F L Y I R T B Q
R B X A U N K N X C M O N K S E A L N K D S
B A R B A R Y M A C A Q U E J G Q K T K E L
I E C Q R O E L T E E B T I M R E H I Z W O
L V D B A L K A N S N O W V O L E R V P X W
L X W E R H S Y R A N A C Y M O G V X U D F
```

Angel Shark	Corsican Hare	Marbled Polecat
Apollo Butterfly	Desman	Mink
Atlantic Cod	Eurasian Lynx	Monk Seal
Balkan Snow Vole	European Eel	Pika
Barbary Macaque	Ground Squirrel	Western Gerbil
Brown Bear	Hermit Beetle	Wild Goat
Canary Shrew	Long Eared Bat	

The answers are on page 217.

5. The Future History of Climate Change

Dad arrived home about the same time as they did. As Heath parked his car at the kerb outside the house, Dad's car whirred past them and into the garage, with Dad waving and smiling from the window. He was always happy, Jake knew, to have the family all together for dinner. It happened less and less often these days, now that Heath was living away from home.

Heath pressed the button to release the seat belts and open the doors, and they all clambered out of the car – Jake a little more reluctantly than usual. He had *hugely* enjoyed the ride home in the back seat next to Sarah. Every time they turned sharply or hit a speed bump, he 'accidentally' slid closer to her, until their elbows were almost touching. After they had dropped Heath's friend Tom off halfway, Heath had asked if he wanted to sit up front. Jake said – a little too quickly, perhaps – that he was fine where he was. He wondered if that was too obvious. For her part, Sarah didn't seem to mind any of it. Result!

But now they were home, and Jake's thoughts turned back to his project, and the final subject that needed discussing – the history of climate change. He had learned a lot over the last two days, but much of it was still all muddled up in his head. He now understood fairly well *what* had happened, but didn't really know *when*. Yet he still had to build his timeline of climate-change events. Heath and Sarah weren't much use for that – they were only ten years older than he was, so weren't around when it all kicked off.

He hoped that Mum and Dad would help him sort it all out over dinner. They'd know. They were *old*.

Inside the house Dad was already preparing dinner in the kitchen, while Mum was attempting to wrestle Elise into her high chair. Elise squirmed and giggled, clearly enjoying the game. Mum apparently was enjoying it a lot less. As Heath, Sarah and Jake entered the room, she was frowning and biting her tongue in concentration.

'Hi, Mum,' said Heath.

'Hi, Heath. Hello, Sarah – nice to see you,' she said, managing a quick glance and smile before turning her eyes back to the task at hand.

'Hi, Mrs Sherill,' said Sarah, 'Can I, err, help with anything?'

'If the two of you could . . . give Dad a hand . . . laying the table,' she said, still struggling with Elise's flailing arms and legs, '. . . that'd be great. I've kind of got my hands full here . . . '

'Will do,' said Heath, making for the kitchen cabinets to find some plates. 'What are we having?'

'Cricket chips and spicy Beetle Burgers,' replied Dad, 'with some veggies on the side. Then strawberry choc ices for afters.'

'Alllll right!' said Jake.

'You finished with your project yet, Jake?' said Dad, shoving a tray full of raw black Beetle Burger patties into the pulse oven and jabbing the button to fire it up.

'Getting there,' said Jake. 'Just one bit left to research – the history and politics stuff. Then I have to write it all up. Can I talk to you and Mum about it now, so that I can do it after dinner?'

'Fire away,' said Dad. 'The burgers will only be about five minutes, but we can chat while we eat.'

'Great,' said Jake. He grabbed his laptop from his bag, plonked himself into a seat at the dinner table and pressed the button to switch it on. 'Computer,' he said flatly, 'open new document – title: "Climate-Change Project" – record speech as type.'

The computer bleeped in response, and the display instantly changed to show a blank white page. The title 'Climate-Change Project' sat above a blinking cursor near the top.

'OK,' said Jake, 'so when did all this climate-change stuff begin?'

On the screen before him, the computer recorded and displayed the words as he spoke, but recognizing the interview format, it helpfully deleted the 'OK' and 'so' at the beginning.

'Actually, it was quite a long time ago,' answered Dad. 'If you're talking about the greenhouse effect, it's been going on for billions of years, for most of the Earth's history. But we only discovered it around 200 years ago, in the mid-nineteenth century.' The computer typed on, happily recording words and numbers so that Jake could find them easily later on.

'What about actual global warming and climate change?' said Jake. 'Not the natural stuff – the unnatural stuff, which we caused ourselves?'

'Well, that started happening around the same time – at the end of the nineteenth century, after the Industrial Revolution brought steam engines, coal and other fossil fuels into our daily lives. But it wasn't until the 1930s that scientists began to notice trends in global warming that were linked to burning coal, oil, gas and petroleum. And it wasn't until the 1970s that scientists really began to worry about the long-term effects of warming on our lives.'

'So after that we started taking notice?'

'Not quite,' answered Mum, spooning a lump of gooey yellow baby food into Elise's open mouth. 'There was a lot of confusion, and the scientists and governments didn't really get their act together until the eighties and nineties. It was only then that the United Nations created a special climate-change committee group and drew up the first treaty for cutting carbon emissions.'

'The Kyoto thingy, right?'

'The Kyoto Protocol, yes. It was created in 1997, and most of the world signed it.'

'And you and Dad remember that?'

'Jake! That was over half a century ago! Of course we don't remember it – we weren't even born yet. How old do you think we are? Wait – don't answer that. Look – we learned about it from our parents, and in school, just like you are, OK?'

'OK, OK,' said Jake, 'chill out. I don't care how old and crumbly you are.'

Across the table, Sarah and Heath exchanged looks and tried not to laugh as they put out the plates and cutlery.

Mum sighed. 'Anyway,' she continued, 'that was far from the end of it. Even though the treaty was there, most people – and most countries – just weren't that serious about sticking to it.

'Governments and environmental groups tried hard to raise awareness through information campaigns about recycling, saving energy and cutting carbon footprints . . . things like that. But the world had yet to see the damage and the danger. And you couldn't really expect people to change their lifestyles voluntarily, spend more money and put up with new hardships if they didn't have that much to begin with. So it wasn't until things started getting ugly – and new, international laws and rules were made – that people started changing their ways for the greater good of the planet.'

'OK – dinner's ready,' called Dad, bringing a platter of steaming burgers in buns and crispy triangular chips from the kitchen. Jake grabbed a burger and a handful of cricket chips, cramming a few into his mouth before they reached his plate.

'What do you mean, "getting ugly"?' Jake asked through half a mouthful of crispy insect.

'Well,' said Dad, taking up the theme, 'in 2009 a group of scientists released a paper declaring that the world was close to disaster, since we were already close to several ecological "tipping points".'

'Tipping points?' said Jake.

'Like thresholds or limits, past which there would be no going back. Like the polar ice sheets. Once a certain amount of the ice had melted, they said, the rest would disappear within a year or two, and there would be no going back. Along with melting ice sheets, carbon emissions and deforestation, they also pointed to nitrogen pollution, freshwater pollution, and other factors that might soon spell doom for the lot of us.'

'Whoa. Heavy,' said Jake, biting into his Beetle Burger with relish. He was genuinely concerned by his dad's serious words. But nothing could stop him from enjoying his favourite meal in the whole universe.

'Indeed,' said Dad. 'Then in 2010 a huge oil spill in the Gulf of Mexico made a lot of people in America take more notice of the damage that drilling for oil was doing to the environment.

Eventually this led to new laws and taxes concerning oil drilling, energy use and carbon emissions.'

'Once the biggest polluter in the world had done this,' said Mum, 'it was hard for other countries – like China, Russia, India and the newly formed UNASUR – not to follow. By 2020 the world had agreed to limit carbon emissions with caps and taxes, and to cut carbon emissions by 80% by the year 2050.'

'And it worked?' asked Jake, polishing off his burger and hoovering the remaining cricket chips from his plate.

'Well, here we are,' said Dad. 'In the end the carbon caps helped to drive the development of alternative energies, and the world managed to cut emissions by an average of 85%. Not bad at all. And now, with the nuclear fusion just being developed, it looks like we might soon cut them by 100% – to zero emissions, forever. All in all, it's a pretty exciting time to be alive! Now who wants a strawberry choc ice?'

'Me!' said Jake, immediately embarrassed at his kid-like outburst in front of Sarah.

Heath laughed and stood up. 'I'll get them,' he said.

As Jake swallowed the last bite of his choc ice, feeling the sweet, sticky liquid cool his throat as it slid down, he thought hard about what his dad had just said.

The world, Jake realized, seemed somehow different. It seemed brighter today than it had only yesterday morning. Maybe it was the car ride home with Sarah. Maybe it was the choc ice. Or maybe it was the time he had spent with his whole family – just talking, listening, learning about their lives and their thoughts. Or maybe he just appreciated the world and his life all the more, now he knew it might have turned out so differently.

'Well, one thing's for certain,' said Jake, 'I'm glad you old folks got it sorted when you did. Otherwise we wouldn't have any of this to enjoy here today.'

Mum and Dad looked shocked. Jake had never come out with anything this deep or thoughtful before. Sarah sat smiling at him from the seat beside his. Then suddenly she leaned over and kissed his cheek. 'You are the smartest little boy I know,' she said.

Jake's face burned, and he was too giddy even to mind her calling him a 'little boy'. He looked across the table at Heath, fully expecting a barrage of teasing comments about his glowing face. But Heath was smiling too.

'Here,' he said, extending a hand, 'just for that, you can have my choc ice too. Might help cool you down.'

'Errr, thanks,' said Jake, rising from the table, 'but can you stick it in the freezer for me? I'm off to write this thing up. I'll have it when I'm done.'

He hefted his laptop and made for the stairs. At the bottom, he spun back to face them once more.

'Thanks, guys,' he said. 'I'm really grateful for everything you've done. Everything.' And with that he turned and bounded up the stairs to his bedroom, leaving his parents still stunned and silent behind him.

Yep – even with homework to do, the world wasn't such a bad place after all . . .

Getting Serious

We have known about the greenhouse effect and the possibilities of climate change for over a century. But it's only recently that the whole world has started taking it very seriously. In spite of all the evidence that scientists have produced for climate change, confusion and misinformation have cast doubt over it for decades.

Today, while a few continue to stall and dither, most of the world's nations are taking it very seriously indeed. People and governments worldwide are coming together, taking action and taking steps to tackle climate change head-on.

Have we really known about it that long?

In one way or another, yes.

The idea of atmospheric warming goes back to the mid-nineteenth century. It was then that famous physicists Joseph Fourier and John Tyndall discovered that the Earth – given its distance from the Sun – is much warmer than it really should be, and that this was probably due to certain gases in the atmosphere that could block or trap infrared radiation.

At around that time, we began adding huge amounts of these 'greenhouse' gases (in the form of carbon dioxide) to the atmosphere, as the coal and steam-powered machines of the Industrial Revolution appeared in factories and on railways around the world. And by 1896 Swedish scientist Svante Arrhenius had published the first calculation of how much global warming was likely to happen thanks to emissions from this new coal-fired technology.

So even then, we knew for sure that we were causing global warming and climate change?

No, not quite. While a few scientists had some idea of it, everyday people in the factories and on the trains had no idea that they were so drastically altering the world they lived in.

It wasn't until the 1930s that a few scientists began talking about visible trends of global warming in the atmosphere. And it wasn't until the 1960s and 1970s that they described what would happen if that warming was to melt glaciers and polar ice sheets, raise sea levels, or alter weather patterns for the worse. Once all *that* was out in the open, the world began to take more notice.

So what happened then?

By 1988 over 180 countries within the United Nations took these warnings seriously enough to form the *Intergovernmental Panel on Climate Change*, or IPCC. Over the next two decades the IPCC put together research from scientists around the globe, and reported back to the United Nations with their findings and recommendations. Their first report was made in 1992, and the very same year 166 countries signed an agreement to look at their greenhouse-gas emissions and start working out how to cut them down. This was called the *United Nations Framework Convention on Climate Change* (or UNFCCC). It was signed by almost every nation in the UN, including Britain, France, Russia, China, Australia and the United States of America.

Well, that sounds pretty serious to me.

It was. And just five years later, in 1997, the same nations met in Kyoto in Japan to share what they had discovered, and to plan the *Kyoto Protocol* – an agreement to make serious cuts in the amounts of greenhouse gases (especially carbon dioxide) released by each nation. By 2005 the Kyoto Protocol had been signed by over 140 countries.

But with all this going on, why are people still talking about whether or not climate change really exists?

Well, while the vast majority of the scientific world agrees that human-caused climate change is real (and well under way), the science is complicated and tricky to describe. Even among climate scientists, long-range predictions of how much warming will happen (and when) can vary quite a bit. So many people are understandably still confused.

Other people are convinced that 90% of the world's expert scientists are just plain wrong, and – in spite of the evidence – climate change either does not exist, or isn't a problem worth dealing with.

But perhaps the biggest reason why people still doubt the existence of climate change (rather than what should be done about it) is not that they're confused or sceptical. It's because they've been misled.

Misled? Like, *lied* to?

Unfortunately, yes. In the late 1980s – right after the IPCC was formed – a number of big oil and gas companies got together to form their *own* climate-change panel.

In short, these companies stood to lose a *lot* of money if the world decided to limit the buying and burning of fossil fuels. So this 'Global Climate Coalition' was designed to convince the media, politicians and individuals that climate-change science was 'too uncertain' to be worth worrying about. And whether they were right or wrong, their reports and news articles had a huge effect on how people now view climate science and climate change.

But that's just crazy. You could have all the money in the world, and it'd be useless if you had no world to live in and nothing to spend it on.

That's very true. And thankfully, since then, even these big oil and gas companies (or most of them, at least) have come to realize this. Many of them have even joined the effort to combat climate change – spending billions of pounds each year to develop alternative energy technologies and to find cleaner, more efficient ways of burning fossil fuels.

Well, if they can change their minds, I suppose anyone can.

Right. And as more evidence appears for climate change – and more people realize just how expensive or disastrous it would be to ignore it – more and more of the doubters and deniers are changing their minds too.

After decades of research, discussion and argument, the twenty-first century is one in which people are *serious* about the perils of human-caused climate change.

Now we just have to agree what to do about it . . .

New Rules for a New World

In 2009 a group of expert environmental scientists published a warning to the world. The planet, they said, was close to its limit. Or, more accurately, close to *several* limits.

While the Earth will go on without us, there's only so much humankind can take. And if we get too far beyond certain boundaries for climate change, deforestation, pollution and species loss, the future of human civilization will be very bleak indeed.

The bad news is that three of those boundaries – for species loss, nitrogen pollution and climate change – have already been crossed. But the good news is, there's still time to put things straight and get ourselves back within safe limits for living. We can set new rules to limit the damage we do, and to ensure we're living in ways that won't destroy the planet for our descendants.

Are we really going to destroy the entire planet?!

Well, not the planet itself, no. The Earth itself will most likely live on long after we're gone. It's been around for over 4 billion years, and human civilization has only lived on it for the last few thousand of them. No, it's not the planet that needs saving. It's *us*.

So what are we saving ourselves from? Climate change?
Among other things, yes.

Other things?
As we've already learned, climate change *is* one major problem facing our world. If the climate keeps changing, then before too long much of humankind will be facing drought, famine, disease and destructive weather. But there are other problems too. (Some of which are linked to climate change, others not.) And if we're not careful, we might be facing some of *these* problems even sooner.

Like what?
The first three, we've met already.

Biodiversity loss (or species loss) due to climate change – and other causes such as habitat destruction – is happening at 100–1,000 times the natural rate. If this continues or worsens, whole fishing and farming systems could collapse, leaving the natural world impoverished and millions of people without food.

Ocean acidification – caused by chemical pollution, the burning of fossil fuels and the release of excess carbon dioxide into the atmosphere – is threatening to destroy coral reefs and marine ecosystems around the world. Again, if this goes on, many marine animals (and fishing stocks) could disappear within decades.

And as world *freshwater use* grows, many of the world's

lakes, rivers and freshwater ecosystems will vanish altogether by the end of the century. With them, the freshwater supplies of perhaps hundreds of villages, towns and cities will vanish too. To say nothing of the impact on animal ecosystems.

That's no good. And there's more?

Unfortunately so. Aside from these big, hefty problems, there's also *ozone depletion* and *nitrogen pollution*.

Atmospheric ozone pollution – made famous by the 'hole in the ozone layer' spotted by scientists during the 1980s – has been a problem for a while. It's caused by the release of gassy chemicals (typically from aerosol sprays and refrigerators) that destroy the oxygen-rich ozone layer in the Earth's high atmosphere.

This layer shields us from harmful ultraviolet radiation emitted by the Sun, and without it many plants and animals (including us) would suffer from radiation damage or radiation-linked diseases such as skin cancer. And while the world has taken steps to limit it – by getting rid of ozone-destroying chemicals called chlorofluorocarbons (or CFCs), there are *other* chemicals still being released which are doing damage up there.

The other big planetary problem, *nitrogen pollution*, is caused by the overuse of nitrogen-containing plant fertilizers, which get washed from farm soils into lakes, rivers and oceans. As nitrogen builds up in these places, it causes huge blooms of algae, which suck the oxygen from the water, creating huge watery 'dead zones' that suffocate fish, plants and other organisms. This obviously isn't good news for future biologists or fishermen either.

So while these latter two problems aren't really linked to

climate change, they are big issues we will have to tackle if we're to preserve our way of life beyond the next century.

How do we tackle 'em?

First, we do more research to work out how bad things have got, and how best we can get back to where we should be. Then we agree global rules and limits that will help shift the world back within safe boundaries for living.

We can tackle ozone depletion and nitrogen pollution by finding alternatives to the destructive chemicals and fertilizers that cause them, and then limiting or banning the deadly culprits. We can tackle biodiversity loss by putting limits on the destruction of plant and natural animal habitat. By creating global nature reserves (on land and at sea) we can help safeguard plant and animal species and fish stocks for future generations.

But perhaps the most important step we can take is to make the shift from fossil fuels to renewable energy sources. All at once this would slow the rate of climate change, ocean acidification and biodiversity loss and make the damaging effects of the other problems far easier to deal with.

Shoving the World Towards Cleaner Energy

Right now the world gets less than 3% of its energy from clean, renewable energy sources like solar, wind and hydropower. Most of the rest we get from burning fossil fuels, which flood the atmosphere and oceans with carbon dioxide, accelerating climate change and destroying marine environments. So we desperately need to make the switch to renewable fuels as soon as possible.

The trouble is, we simply cannot do it yet. Even if we all stopped using fossil fuels tomorrow, renewable energy technologies – as they are today – could not make up the shortfall and supply all the energy the world needs. And as long as coal, oil and gas remain so much cheaper than their renewable alternatives, there's little hope of people, businesses and nations making that switch.

The world is stuck in an energy rut, and the only way to shove ourselves out is by making carbon emissions –

and fossil fuels – more *expensive*. Only then will we get the cheap, clean energy we need.

Hold on – now I'm *really* confused. How does making one fuel more expensive make another one cheaper?

It doesn't. Not right away, at least. But depending on how you do it, it could encourage the world to shift from expensive, dirty fuels to expensive, clean ones. Or at the very least, it'll encourage engineers to find ways of making cheap, dirty fuels into cheap, clean ones.

Huh? You've totally lost me there.

All right, let's try this – a little thought experiment to help you see it all more clearly.

Imagine you live on the Moon or on Mars. You, your friends and everyone you know live within a huge sealed bio-dome, with no access to the outside. Everybody lives in groovy electric space-igloos, which are arranged in circles that spread from the centre outwards. Beyond these are larger buildings – factories that produce food, clothing and other goods for the igloo-dwellers, and power plants that produce electricity to power all the igloos, vehicles and machines in the dome.

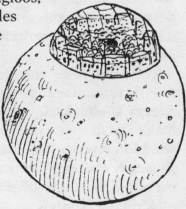

OK. So now what?

Now, all the waste produced within the dome – from the

factories, power plants and igloos – has to go *somewhere*, right? Since you can't just stick it out for the bin men.

Right. So where does it go?

Imagine there's a huge tank, set into a circular pit in the very centre of the dome, and everyone lobs their waste (food scraps, chemical sludge, waste water from sinks and toilets – everything) into that pit. Inside the tank, billions of genetically engineered bacteria slowly break the waste down and turn it into a liquid goo that sinks, through a small hole in the bottom, into the lunar (or Martian) soil.

Now as long as you don't add *too much* waste *too quickly*, it all works beautifully. But if you add *too much waste at once*, the super-bacteria can't break it down quickly enough, and the waste starts to spill out of the top of the pit. From there it spreads out and contaminates the surrounding igloos. The exposed waste releases heat as it rots, the dome gets hot and stinky, everyone gets ill and you have to abandon the dome.

OK . . . so what's the problem?

The problem is that the pit can only handle 100 bags of waste per week. And while each igloo only lobs in one or two bags, the factories and power plants are chucking in *thousands* of bags of waste every week. So what do you do?

You dig a bigger pit.

You can't. There's no room. The pit you've got is all you have.

All right, then, you just make the factories and power plants cut down on their waste.

Say they're allowed only 10 bags of waste each every week.

Good idea! But unfortunately, cutting their waste down from 1,000-plus bags a week to 10 bags means changing the way they make their products. Which makes the food and electricity they supply about twice as expensive as before. Now the igloo-dwellers can't afford to heat their homes, power their space-ovens or buy food to cook in them. So instead of everyone getting hot and sick, now they're all freezing and starving. FAIL.

What?! That's not fair. So we can't win. We're done for.

Not necessarily. How about this – rather than tell the factories and power plants to cut down to 10 bags a week, we tell them they can dump up to 50 bags. But for every bag over the original 10-bag limit, they have to pay each igloo 100 space-dollars. Now the costs of food and energy go up a little (but not as much as before), but all the igloo-dwellers have a little extra cash to buy it with, so it's OK.

But with a limit of 50 each, won't they still be dumping too many bags for the pit to handle?

Not for long. Because it's now getting expensive for the factories and power plants to dump waste, they'll be trying to find ways of cutting the number of bags down to 10 or less anyway, so they won't have to pay anyone at all. Plus, every year, we'll reduce the 50-bag maximum limit by 10 bags, and the 10-bag 'free dumpage' allowance by 1 bag.

Before long, we'll be down to our happy, 10-bag-per-factory limit. Better yet, in an effort to cut costs, the factories and power plants would probably have found ways of dumping even less than that. Perhaps they'd make their food and energy production so efficient that they could create less than 5 bags of waste each week, and pay the igloos hardly anything. Or maybe they'd even find ways of recycling *all* their waste – producing food and energy for the whole dome without creating *any* waste at all.

Ohhh — now I think I get it. So the dome represents the whole world, right? And we're dumping waste into it too quickly?
Exactly. The waste bags represents *tonnes of carbon emissions* (from burning fossil fuels in homes, factories and power plants), and the pit represents the *atmosphere* and *oceans*. We can dump only so much, because the atmosphere and oceans *can't get any bigger*, and there's *only so much carbon they can absorb* before the environment is ruined.

. . . and as long we keep treating the atmosphere and oceans like a rubbish dump, we're basically asking for trouble.
Spot on, yes. And since we can't yet produce all our food and energy through recycling (or renewable) technology, we must – at the very least – slow down our rate of dumpage. We have to put a *cap* (or maximum level) on the total amount of carbon waste the world is allowed to dump into the air each year.

But if that cap is too small, then everything will get too expensive and everybody will be miserable?

Right. So just like with the waste bags in the dome, we should set the cap quite high at first, then make it smaller over time. This – along with forcing the factories and energy producers (and users) to pay a *tax* on waste-creating fossil fuels – will encourage everyone to develop less wasteful methods of creating the energy, food and products we need.

If we make carbon emissions expensive, then that will give us *all* a reason to clean up our act. Over time, it should lead to a future in which fossil-fuel technologies will be changed to make them cleaner (and so cheaper) to produce and use.

At the same time, renewable energy sources producing hardly any carbon emissions at all will be free from the wasteful 'carbon emissions tax', and they'll become as cheap as (or even cheaper than) the pricier fossil-fuel alternatives. When this happens, the world's energy companies will be rushing to develop new and better renewable energy technologies, and the people of the world will be rushing to buy and use them.

Of course, it'd be great if they just did that, anyway . . .

Right. But the world is a pricey place to live, and it's hard for people to do what's good for the future world when they're struggling to get by in the present one. All they need is to see the big picture, and to understand that we can't all keep dumping our waste into the world forever. And perhaps a gentle shove in the right direction . . .

The World Works Together

If we are all to survive beyond the next century, the countries and peoples of the world must work *together* as we never have before. The huge, global problems of the twenty-first century simply can't be solved without huge, global efforts.

We have to change the world's energy systems, protect and re-grow our forests and change the way we farm, fish, use water and use land. None of that will be possible with people and nations sitting on the sidelines. If it's going to work, everyone must do their part. And perhaps most importantly, we all have to agree to just *slow down* a bit. To slow the relentless growth of farms, cities and human populations that is pushing our planet to its limits.

Can we really *do* all that?

We can, and we will. Because we *have to*. Eventually the problems will get so bad that the world will start working together out of pure desperation – to try to save what's left. But hopefully people around the world will have a bit more sense than that, and will start tackling the problems sooner rather than later. In fact, many global efforts to combat climate change and conserve the environment are already under way. This is a good sign. All we have to do now is get *everyone* involved and step up the efforts until things get under control.

Like carbon emissions and climate change?

Right. As we've already seen, that's the biggie. The world needs an entirely new energy system – one based on low-carbon, renewable energy sources and fuels. And the only way that's going to happen is if we convince enough people that it needs to be done, and *all* work together to make it happen. It's no use one country going all 'green' and decreasing its carbon emissions to zero . . .

. . . if another one is building more coal-fired power stations and releasing enough carbon for *two* countries, right?

Exactly. Countries will have to be stricter with each other, making new rules for carbon emissions (like the carbon 'cap' we met on page 203) and making sure everyone sticks to their limits. Limiting, taxing and trading carbon emissions, as we've seen, is the best way of encouraging a *worldwide* shift to less wasteful low-carbon energy sources. Done properly, experts reckon this could decrease global carbon emissions by up to 80% by the year 2050. But it'll only work if *everyone* sticks to their carbon limits and pays their carbon taxes.

And the same goes for chopping down forests and stuff?

Yep – same story. It's no use Brazil agreeing to stop or slow the clearing of its rainforests, if on the other side of the world Indonesia is stepping up its logging and land clearance for farmers. There will need to be globally agreed rules about land development and deforestation, and those who break them will need to be punished (say, by banning imports of wood or paper until they agreed to stop logging in protected areas).

This will be tough in developing countries, where populations are growing fast and more land is needed to support them. But that doesn't mean it shouldn't be done. If forests are protected and new land development is limited, then people will be encouraged to find better, more efficient ways of farming and living. This might include developing high-efficiency farming methods for use in smaller land areas. Or perhaps farms in cities – like the 'vertical farms' we met on page 165.

So if we do all that, we'll solve all our problems?

That will certainly help, but it probably won't fix everything.

We'd also have to learn – as a planet – to make better use of the limited land and resources we *do* have. In particular, we'd have to make new rules to change the way farms and factories use water.

More than 70% of the world's fresh water is used to irrigate crops and feed livestock, yet around one-third of that water is wasted – evaporating from fields or leaking from troughs and hoses. Meanwhile, factories worldwide waste up to 88% of the huge amounts of fresh water they draw from wells each year and are responsible for most of the world's freshwater pollution.

So we put limits on wasting water?

Better yet, we put limits on the total amount of water they're allowed to draw from wells and aquifers. Then it's up to them to plug the leaks and find more efficient ways of using water for farming and manufacturing. And, of course, we enforce strict global laws on water pollution, as *nobody* wants that.

But perhaps the most important thing we can do is to slow the runaway growth of the human world. No one likes to talk about it, but the truth is that the growth of human populations around the world – along with our increasingly wasteful lifestyles – is the one thing that makes all of our other problems worse.

How's that?

It creates too many taps for the amount of water we have. It adds millions of cars and houses, increasing the carbon emissions and pollution that are destroying our atmosphere and environment. And it makes too many mouths to feed, requiring more food, more farming, more land development and more deforestation.

But we can't stop people from having children, can we? That doesn't seem right . . .

No, no one wants to stop people from having families if they want them. But we can help solve some of the problems that make many people in developing countries feel like they *must* have large families, just to survive.

In the developing parts of Africa and Asia – where populations are growing fastest – people often have lots of children because they need the help with farming or other work. But in these same places, fewer children survive to become adults, as poor healthcare and hospitals mean childhood diseases and deaths are much more common. So people have big families partly to ensure they have *some* children to help support them as they get older.

What can we do about that?

We – in the developed world – can come together to help improve healthcare in developing countries, by training doctors and supplying them with cheap medicines. With better education and healthcare, and fewer childhood deaths, parents can choose to have fewer children. Over time, this slows population growth, and relieves the pressure on water, land and other resources.

Would that really work?

Yep. It has already happened in western Europe, where population growth in most countries has now stopped or reversed.

But again, this all depends upon everyone working together. Without that, nothing much can be done, and the world will keep growing, out of control.

Only if all countries work together, as one, can we strike the balance between the human world and the environment we live in and depend on.

We've only got one planet, one home. It's up to us to keep it clean, repair the damage we've done, and keep it safe for future generations. Cow farts alone will not destroy the planet. But if we're not careful, our greed and selfishness just might, for us anyway.

If we all chip in and help out, the future should be cool, clean and bright. If we don't, it'll be hot, dirty and stinky.

And nobody wants that, do they?

History of Climate Change – Quiz

Try this tricky multiple-choice quiz, and test your knowledge of climate-change history.

1. The chemical found in fertilizers which pollutes soils, rivers and oceans is called . . .
a) nitrogen
b) oxygen
c) foxygen

2. These natural, underwater habitats are home to thousands of plant and animal species. But they're disappearing worldwide, due to increasing acidity in the oceans. What are they called?
a) islands
b) submarines
c) coral reefs

3. The Swedish scientist who discovered global warming in 1896 was called . . .
a) Svante Arrhenius
b) Smeli Armpitius
c) Dave

4. The layer of gas that surrounds our planet, and shields us from harmful radiation, is called . . .
a) the ozone layer
b) the bozone layer
c) the frozone layer

5. In 1997 the countries of the UN met in Japan and made a plan to cut global greenhouse-gas emissions. In which Japanese city did they meet?
a) Tokyo
b) Kyoto
c) Toto

6. In 1992 how many countries worldwide signed an agreement promising to look at their greenhouse-gas emissions?
a) 3
b) 26
c) 166

7. In the eighteenth century, scientist John Tyndall discovered that the Earth is kept warm by heat trapped in its atmosphere – much like warmth trapped inside a house with glass windows. What is the name he gave to this process?
a) the beanhouse effect
b) the greenhouse effect
c) the spleenhouse effect

8. How much of the world's energy currently comes from renewable sources like solar, wind and hydroelectric power?
a) 3%
b) 10%
c) 90%

The answers are on page 217.

Jake's Story: the Quiz

Just for a final bit of fun, try this last, twenty-question quiz about the story of Jake and his adventures in our future world.

1. What does Jake want to be when he gets older?

2. What is the name of Jake's favourite computer game?

3. What kind of car does Jake's dad drive?

4. What are two types of alternative liquid fuels used by older non-electric cars?

5. How are the lights and gadgets in Jake's house powered?

6. According to Jake's mum, what is the difference between how energy was used before and how it is used now?

7. What is Austin's favourite toy?

8. What happens to the used water from Jake's toilet, sink and shower?

9. Why does Jake's mum like shopping at the farmers' market?

10. What is Jake's favourite dessert?

11. What are two things people don't eat much of any more? Why?

12. What does Heath study at university?

13. What does Sarah study?

14. What type of pet will Jake's mum not let him have?

15. According to Sarah, which insect species were harmed or lost due to climate change?

16. What happened to people as a result of glaciers melting?

17. When did scientists begin to worry about the effects of climate change?

18. When was the Kyoto Protocol signed?

19. What pushed the world to cut carbon emissions?

20. How did Jake feel about his homework assignment after talking to his family?

The answers are on pages 217-18.

Answers

Future Transport – Wordsearch, page 48

```
U Q K Q V I A K I D I Z W R A K W X M T L G
N Y G G Z Q E D S N D Z G M O D N H A E I L
I I R P Z B J L H G E U R O S T A R G S G L
D E A O Y N J Z E B F S M Z F N G A L H G G
Q N S R Y M T A L C I J N L F N T Y E A N X
K M S U T U P K B R T O M A T B T Q V R N X
P K O L V R B Q Y V I R D V K O L I Q O I N
K B L K M G I L A U Y C I I K N S W H A N D
R N I E Q W X A F K V D C E D I O D D G U
E X N O H M B U R M A B L B C S N H H S G C
O F E T O M O N O M O B I L E A E M S T M
M C G E V V Z P E U C A W J J H R L M E L S
O K T W E A C G V W T N X I P J B B D R N U
F N I A R T D E E P S H G I H C L D Q O Z A
```

Power and Energy – Quiz, page 92

1-a, 2-b, 3-c, 4-a, 5-a, 6-b, 7-c, 8-a, 9-b, 10-a

How did you score?

1–2: dead battery

3–5: mild buzzing

6–8: bright spark

9–10: flash of genius

H₂O – Quiz, page 132

1-c, 2-a, 3-b, 4-a, 5-a, 6-b, 7-c, 8-c, 9-a, 10-b

How did you score?

1–2: wet blanket

3–5: ripples of intelligence

6–8: making a splash

9–10: ruler of the (brain) waves

World Population – Puzzle, page 152

Nigeria	A	152 million (8th)
India	C	1.2 billion (2nd)
Indonesia	G	243 million (4th)
USA	I	310 million (3rd)
China	E	1.3 billion (1st)
Brazil	J	201 million (5th)
Bangladesh	F	156 million (7th)
Russia	D	139 million (9th)
Pakistan	B	184 million (6th)
Japan	H	127 million (10th)

Glaciers – Anagrams, page 159

Ururashraju / Peru

Athabasca / Canada

Chacaltaya / Bolivia

Siachen / India

Mer de Glace / France

Aletsch / Switzerland

Imja / Nepal

Grinnell / United States

```
W C O R S I C A N H A R E P G G U T Y R R W
E U R O P E A N E E L N W N B F W R G F A K
S T Q A J G U H K H Z W G I Q D Q F H U E M
T G R O U N D S Q U I R R E L M N N M V B D
E U R A S I A N L Y N X I L L D E S M A N M
R R K T A B D E R A E G N O L S G U M M W Z
N A T L A N T I C C O D K B W E H O L Y O U
G K M T A C E L O P D E L B R A M A A K R D
E X A P O L L O B U T T E R F L Y I R T B Q
R B X A U N K N X C M O N K S E A L N K D S
B A R B A R Y M A C A Q U E J G Q K T K E L
I E C Q R O E L I E E B T I M R E H I Z W O
L V D B A L K A N S N O W V O L E R V P X W
L X W E R H S Y R A N A C Y M O G V X U D F
```

History of Climate Change – Quiz, page 210

1–a, 2–c, 3 a, 4–a, 5–b, 6–c, 7–b, 8–a
How did you score?
1–2: Have you jumped to the quiz before reading the book? Go back and start again.
3–6: If you're going to do your bit for the survival of the planet, you'll have to work a bit harder.
7–8: The future of the planet will be safe in your hands. Give this book to your friends so that they can become as well-informed as you are.

Jake's Story : the Quiz, page 212

1. A games designer.
2. World of Ninja Dragoncraft.

3. A silver Nissan ElectroRailer.
4. Grassoline and biodiesel.
5. By a geothermal generator, Roofmill, solar paint and windows, and a clean nuclear power plant.
6. Before, power flowed in one direction, from power plant to homes and businesses. Now homes and businesses can create power and share it with the plant and their neighbours.
7. The VacuBot.
8. It is cleaned and reused to water the plants and flowers in the garden.
9. It's cheaper and it saves energy buying food that is locally grown.
10. Strawberry choc ices.
11. Cereals and meat. They took too much water and space to produce and were expensive.
12. He uses computer models to study how climate change affects human populations.
13. She studies the effects of climate change on plants, trees and animals.
14. A tarantula.
15. Moths and butterflies.
16. Many people had to leave islands because of flooding, and others had to find new water supplies.
17. In the 1970s.
18. 1997.
19. There was a major oil spill in the US, and the President supported cutting emissions. Other major nations followed.
20. Grateful that he lived in a much improved world.

Index

Why is SNOT green?

The First Science Museum Question and Answer Book

Glenn Murphy

Why is snot green? Do rabbits fart? What is space made of? Where does all the water go at low tide? Can animals talk? What are scabs for? Will computers ever be cleverer than people?

Discover the answers to these and an awful lot of other brilliant questions frequently asked at the Science Museum in this wonderfully funny and informative book.

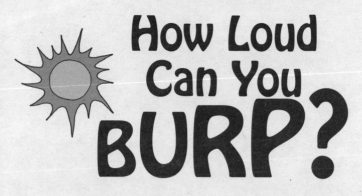

How Loud Can You BURP?

and other extremely important questions (and answers) from the Science Museum

Glenn Murphy

How loud can you burp? Could we use animal poo in power stations to make electricity? Why is water wet, and is anything wetter than water? What's the deadliest disease in the world? What are clouds for?

A second volume of questions and answers from the Science Museum by the author of the mega-bestselling WHY IS SNOT GREEN? A wonderfully funny and informative book with loads of fascinating facts and no boring bits!

Stuff that scares your PANTS off!

The Science Museum Book of Scary Things (and ways to avoid them)

Glenn Murphy

What scares you most? Spiders or sharks?
Ghosts or aliens? Dentists or darkness?

This amazing book takes apart your deepest,
darkest fears. With a bit of biology, a spot of
psychology and oodles of lovely facts and figures,
you'll learn everything there is to know about the
stuff that scares your pants off.